Advance Praise

With his customary lucidity, breadth of learning, and wisdom, Canon Crean here offers insight and spiritual acumen for each week of the year. Scholarly without being stuffy, there is much to commend this volume to any thinking and intelligent Christian.

—The Very Rev. Canon Ian Elliott Davies
Rector, St Thomas the Apostle, Hollywood

Father John Crean is a wonderful spiritual companion—like a good friend sitting across the table who is wise and funny, asking deep questions and listening with the ear of the heart. He is also a scholar who asks inviting questions. He is a perfect companion on the spiritual journey.

—Christopher McCauley
teacher of contemplative spirituality,
retreat, and international pilgrimage leader.

I love that John Crean begins the book by looking at the double meaning of seasons: the passage of time and the flavoring of food. His essays offer flavorful stories and observations that will help us all reflect on how we spend our days, whatever the season.

—Milton Brasher-Cunningham
Author of *The Color of Together:
Mixed Metaphors of Connectedness*

Each of the artful, short reflections points beyond what is measured temporally to what is not, beyond what is to what is not yet, and beyond time altogether to what is eternal. *Week by Week* is the product of a rare author, someone who is both as deeply grounded in Christian tradition as one can imagine but at the same time has the profound ability to touch others with insights of practical depth. The book is the product of mystic and pastor bound together in a most unassuming package, whose words are well worth pondering.

—The Rt Rev Stacy Sauls,
Bishop of the Episcopal Church

How does scripture speak to our twenty-first-century lives? This enduring question is brought to light in this fine book of commentary. John Crean is a priest, theologian, biblical scholar, and Benedictine Oblate. But most of all, he is simply a man whose heart beats with a deep desire for God. He brings to this work the intention for self-awareness and desire for deeper union with the Divine Presence and shares it in a way that is inviting for all. This book reads both like a daily devotional as well as a resource for exploration into important topics in life. Crean weaves in wisdom teaching from scripture and does it with the brilliance and humility that one would expect from one who is steeped in monastic charism.

— Brother Dennis Gibbs
Community of Divine Love

WEEK BY WEEK

Through the Seasons of Life

JOHN EDWARD CREAN, JR.

WEEK BY WEEK

Through the Seasons of Life

JOHN EDWARD CREAN, JR.

Torchflame Books

Copyright © 2023 John Edward Crean, Jr.

Week by Week: Through the Seasons of Life
John Edward Crean, Jr.
jecreanjr@gmail.com
www.jecjr.org

Published 2023, by Torchflame Books

SAN: 920-9298

Paperback ISBN: 978-1-61153-521-1
E-book ISBN: 978-1-61153-522-8
Library of Congress Control Number: 2023901357

ALL RIGHTS RESERVED
No part of this publication may be reproduced, stored in a retrieval system, or transmitted in any form or by any means, electronic, mechanical, photocopying, recording, scanning, or otherwise, except as permitted under Section 107 or 108 of the 1976 International Copyright Act, without the prior written permission except in brief quotations embodied in critical articles and reviews.

Unless otherwise noted, scripture texts in this work are taken from the New American Bible, revised edition© (NABRE) 2010, 1991, 1986, 1970 Confraternity of Christian Doctrine, Washington, D.C. and are used by permission of the copyright owner. All Rights Reserved.

Scripture quotations marked (AMP) are taken from the Amplified Bible, Copyright © 2015 by The Lockman Foundation. Used by permission. https://www.lockman.org.

Scripture quotations marked (CJB) are taken from the COMPLETE JEWISH BIBLE, Copyright© 1998 by David H. Stern. Published by Jewish New Testament Publications, Inc. www.messianicjewish.net. Distributed by Messianic Jewish Resources Int'l. www.messianicjewish.net. All rights reserved. Used by permission.

Scripture quotations marked EHV are from the Holy Bible, Evangelical Heritage Version ® (EHV ®) © 2017 Wartburg Project, Inc. All rights reserved. Used by permission.

Scripture quotations marked (GW) are taken from GOD'S WORD® Copyright© 1995 by God's Word to the Nations. All rights reserved.

Scripture quotations marked (KJV) are taken from the KING JAMES VERSION, public domain.

Scripture quotations marked (MSG) are taken from THE MESSAGE, copyright © 1993, 2002, 2018 by Eugene H. Peterson. Used by permission of NavPress, represented by Tyndale House Publishers. All rights reserved.

Scripture quotations marked (NAB) are taken from the NEW AMERICAN BIBLE© 2010, 1991, 1986, 1970 Confraternity of Christian Doctrine, Washington, D.C. and are used by permission of the copyright owner. All Rights Reserved. No part of the New American Bible may be reproduced in any form without permission in writing from the copyright owner.

Scripture quotations marked (NASB) are taken from the NEW AMERICAN STANDARD BIBLE(r), Copyright (c) 1960,1962,1963,1968,1971,1972,1973,1975,1977 by The Lockman Foundation. Used by permission. https://www.lockman.org.

Scripture quotations marked (NIV) are taken from THE HOLY BIBLE, NEW INTERNATIONAL VERSION®. Copyright© 1973, 1978, 1984, 2011 by Biblica, Inc.™. Used by permission of Zondervan

Scripture quotations marked (NLT) are taken from the Holy Bible, New Living Translation, copyright ©1996, 2004, 2015 by Tyndale House Foundation. Used by permission of Tyndale House Publishers, Carol Stream, Illinois 60188. All rights reserved.

Scripture quotations marked (NRSV) are taken from the New Revised Standard Version Bible, copyright © 1989 the Division of Christian Education of the National Council of the Churches of Christ in the United States of America. Used by permission. All rights reserved.

Scripture quotations marked (PME) are taken from the PHILLIPS MODERN ENGLISH BIBLE, by J. B. Phillips, "The New Testament in Modern English", Copyright© 1962 edition, published by HarperCollins.

Scripture quotations marked (TLB) are taken from The Living Bible copyright © 1971. Used by permission of Tyndale House Publishers, Carol Stream, Illinois 60188. All rights reserved.

For my wife,
the Reverend Canon Charleen Crean,
who has inspired, supported, and sustained me
for almost forty years.

Companions in ministry
and partners for life,
every day we get to spend together
brings blessings upon blessings.

Thank you, my love,
for all you are for our family and me!

"Many are the women of proven worth,
but you have excelled them all." —Proverbs 31:29

SOLOMON'S PRAYER FOR WISDOM

May God grant
that I speak with judgment
and have thoughts worthy
of what I have received,
for God is the guide even of wisdom
and the corrector of the wise.
For both we and our words
are in God's hand,
as are all understanding
and skill in crafts[1].

---

[1] Wisdom 7:15-16 (RSV).

Contents

Introduction xiii
Abandoned 1
Abundance 6
Accessibility 10
Adolescence 14
Anxiety 18
Appearance 24
Asking 30
Baptism 35
Body 39
Bookends 43
Calling 49
Changing 54
Disciplinarian 58
Doubt 62
Emptying 66
Eternity 73
Expletives 76
Fickleness 81
Forgiveness 86
Freedom 91
Fruitfulness 96
Generosity 101
Housecleaning 105
Identity 110
Interviews 114

Joy	119
Knowledge	124
Leave	129
Liberation	133
Life	137
Light	142
Love	148
Motion	154
Naming	159
Nature	164
Obedience	167
Refreshment	171
Repentance	174
Roses	179
Sacraments	183
Shining	187
Shrines	192
Silence	197
Snakes	201
Stewardship	205
Strangers	209
Transfiguration	212
Truth	216
Understanding	220
Unexpected	225
Vision	229
Visiting	234
Some Final Thoughts and Prayers	240
About the Author	241

INTRODUCTION

SEASONS AND SEASONING

Whenever I hear the word *seasoning*, I think of spices such as tarragon, thyme or nutmeg. But I wouldn't have the foggiest idea how to navigate a spice rack. My Proverbs 31 wife, however, has an impressive cabinet chock-full of spices with names I couldn't pronounce much less know what they're for. But she's what I'd call a *seasoned* chef.[1] She knows exactly how to make the otherwise bland tasty. Her cabinet reminds me of an old-fashioned *apothecary*, what today is called a *compounding pharmacy*. Apothecaries looked nothing like nationwide pharmacies. They were chemist's shops which custom-blended pharmaceuticals to craft medicines exactly as prescribed.

Might there be something like a *spiritual* apothecary? Where can I go to get the right spiritual medicine which I might need from time to time?

Compounding pharmacies have multiple cabinets containing myriad medicines. Throughout these pages, let's explore elements that one might find in a *spiritual* apothecary. Let's discover something entirely different. Let's explore how to apply sound theological principles to the

---

1   Pun intended.

challenges of daily life. To borrow a well-known phrase: *Life is Worth Living*.[2] As we navigate the seasons of life, we'll need different remedies for different challenges.

What are the spiritual seasons of life?

I don't know much about meteorology but I know I need a climate with all four seasons. I don't thrive in a flatline climate. I need to sense seasonal variation. Like *meteorological* seasons, there are likewise *spiritual* seasons throughout life. Each provides its own challenge; each calls for its own medicine. Souls, not just bodies, need to be able to adapt, refresh, reboot, and readjust to changing climates. Life is in no sense *monochromatic* but very much *polychromatic*. A hit song once proclaimed *Love is a Many-Splendored Thing*. Life is many-splendored as well, but always challenging, never straight-line.

As we move through the seasons of life, may God's healing power enter to bring us what we need. The Bible does not favor the *lukewarm* life.[3] God isn't thrilled by a bland, nondescript *modus vivendi*. Life is surely worth living, and God came that we might live it to the fullest.[4] God wants more for us than the nondescript.

---

2   A famous TV series by Archbishop Fulton J. Sheen broadcast during the 1950's.
3   Revelation 3: 15-16. "I know your works; I know that you are neither cold nor hot. I wish you were either cold or hot. So, because you are lukewarm, neither hot nor cold, I will spit you out of my mouth."
4   John 10:10.

Abandoned

Imagine this. You're a loyal, faithful, and observant Jewish family. And so, on high holy days such as Passover you don't just want to just celebrate them at your local synagogue. Oh, no. You want to go where the real action is. Skip that little local parish; head for the cathedral!

You're in Israel so of course as an observant, devout Jew, you want to attend the wall-to-wall, jam-packed celebration in the Jerusalem Temple. It would be just as if every Roman Catholic in Italy were to descend on Rome for Holy Week. Great pageantry, mega crowds. So, naturally you bring your whole family. Jewish high holydays are after all family events. For Mary and Joseph their family would have included their pre-teen son, Jesus. Having a twelve-year old in tow—even if he is *Mashiach*, the Messiah—has got to be a challenge in itself.

Remember: Jesus was just about to turn thirteen. He was still obedient,[5] we know, but awfully curious. Soon all the hoopla is over and you're on the way home, but you've made a slight miscalculation. You *assumed* the group from Nazareth was all on board. You *assumed* young Jesus would be among all the others who trekked there and were now homeward bound. Suddenly you realize your teenager is missing! And you've already gone a whole day on foot back to Nazareth.

---

5   Philippians 2:8. "And, having become man, he humbled himself by living a life of utter obedience, even to the extent of dying, and the death he died was the death of a common criminal." (PME).

So, you have no other choice but to turn around and walk all the way back to Temple City. The place is still crawling with hangers-on, lots of people still milling about, well after all the festivities were finished. Jesus is nowhere in sight. Finally, you have nowhere else to turn. You go back to the Temple to pray. As you enter the building, lo and behold, there he is, carrying on an eloquent discourse with the chief rabbis. And what kind of discourse might that be? Jesus isn't asking them about the basics of being a good Jew. He's engaging them about something much more profound. He's challenging them to plumb what the Bible is *really* saying, rather than their punitive, tradition-bound interpretation of it. Mary sighs to herself, "What is he doing? Why did he stay behind? Why didn't he tell us?"

> When his parents saw him, they were astonished; and his mother said to him, "Child, why have you treated us like this? Look, your father and I have been searching for you in great anxiety."[6]

That's the truth all right, *in great anxiety*. Mary was both mad at Jesus for straying from the group as well as scared for his safety. A toxic combination of worries for a concerned young mother. She was angry that he had stayed behind without permission and fearful that something bad, something potentially disastrous might have happened to her son. Remember that earlier Mary had "pondered all these things in her heart."[7] We do not know how fully cognizant she was at that moment about the nature or the destiny of her son.

---

[6] Luke 2: 48. Jesus responds in the very next verse: "Why were you searching for me? Did you not know that I must be in my Father's house?"

[7] Luke 2:19.

On being found, Jesus' response was neither fresh nor sassy. He was just speaking frankly. "Couldn't you have figured out that I'd be in my Father's house?"[8] Jesus had made his own albeit incorrect assumptions. He figured that by now Mary would have fully understood the deeper significance of Gabriel's message. Hers would be no ordinary child but rather the long-awaited *Mashiach*, a man on a mission for all humankind. He would be the one to build upon, build out, and bring to completion the quintessence of the Hebrew Scriptures. The Bible suggests Mary and Joseph's continuing cluelessness about all this.[9] In time, Mary indeed came to grasp the reality of his messiahship in her words at the wedding in Cana.[10] But soon thereafter, the sword Simeon had predicted would slowly begin to tear at the flesh of her sacred heart. Once the Holy Family finally got home to Nazareth from Jerusalem, we are assured that Jesus would become more demonstrably obedient.[11]

Why was Jesus left behind in the first place? Mary and Joseph did not *abandon* him. They just forgot to check on his whereabouts. But I think the teenage Jesus was also kind of hiding out on purpose. He sensed a naturally overpowering attraction to the sanctuary of his *Father's house*. He wasn't drawn there primarily for a scriptural debate with experts. That was a mere byproduct of his presence. Jesus was drawn to the Temple simply to bask in his Father's divine presence. God's sanctuary has its own Godly magnetism, and so of course Jesus felt called to be there, perhaps if for no other reason than to recite these words from Psalm 84:

---

[8] Luke 2:41-52.
[9] Luke 2:50. But they did not understand what he said to them.
[10] John 2:5. His mother said to the servers, "Do whatever he tells you."
[11] Luke 2:52. He grew wiser and older, and became more and more beloved by both God and his fellow human beings (my paraphrase).

> How lovely is your dwelling place,
> O Lord of hosts!
>
> My soul longs, indeed it faints
> for the courts of the Lord;
> my heart and my flesh sing
> for joy to the living God.[12]

Psalms are identified by number and *incipit*, their first Latin words. *Quam dilecta* is the incipit for Psalm. 84. *How beautiful, how delightful, how lovely* all render the sense of *Quam dilecta*. The well-loved hymn tune "Brother James' Air"[13] closely recalls this psalm. Why Jesus stayed behind may be explained by verse nine of this psalm. He wasn't just *left behind* after the Passover festivities. With every fiber of his being, Jesus grasped that:

> One day in your courts is better
> than a thousand in my own room.[14]

Jesus was not ready to go spend the next thousand plus days in his tiny home in Nazareth. He was drawn to linger in *Yahweh's delightful dwelling place*. He didn't want to leave. Had Mary and Joseph not come back to search for him, he would have been just fine. In God the Father's presence, Jesus was totally fulfilled.

Well, how about us? Could you or I honestly say we'd prefer sitting in adoration before the real presence to getting out of church to join the hustle and bustle of what's going on in the world? Which arena is more delightful, more beautiful,

---

[12] Psalm 84:1-2.

[13] *Hymnal 1982: According to the Use of the Episcopal Church* (*Hymnal 1982*) # 517: "How Lovely is thy Dwelling Place, O Lord of Hosts, to me." The *Hymnal 1982* is the primary hymnal of the Episcopal Church in the United States of America.

[14] Psalm 84:9a.

or lovelier to us? Do we attempt to balance contemplation and action in our lives?

At around the age of twelve, on the eve of his *bar mitzvah*, Jesus was steadily growing towards manhood. As a young adult, he was gradually connecting more intentionally with his divinity as well as his mission. By the miracle of his incarnation, Jesus was one *person* possessed of two *natures*, one human and the other divine. We will never be able to fully grasp how his divinity became commingled with his humanity. But as Jesus grew into adolescence and young adulthood, two processes were going on simultaneously within him. His divine nature bound him ever closer to his soul within, while his human nature reached out to care for others.

What draws us? What is the dominant force in my life? Do I strive to balance holiness and helpfulness? Are you and I not likewise called to tarry in the temple, to spend more time with our Lord and faith community? In veiled language, Jesus alluded to his crucifixion:

> And when I am lifted up from the earth, I
> will draw everyone to myself.[15]

Are *you* feeling any particular pull right now? Is the *beauty of holiness* calling out to you? Do you feel the magnetism of the Cross drawing you to your true vocation?

---

[15] John 12:32 (NLT).

Abundance

> I came so that they might have life
> and have it more abundantly.[16]

> My purpose is to give life
> in all its fullness.[17]

Mission statements abound. You find them everywhere. Practically every parish, every business, every political campaign, almost any organized endeavor has its mission statement. But identifying one's own *mission* is not the same thing as coming up with a catchy *slogan*. Mission has to do with *being sent*, as *missionaries* are sent. Businesses sporting *mission statements* have to some degree coopted church-speak, hijacking terminology originally belonging to an entirely different *Weltanschauung*. Companies frequently go on what they term a *retreat*. Companies seeking to revise their *mission* statements are more likely *financially-driven* to do so rather than *purpose-driven*.[18] Borrowing church-speak doubtless serves some useful purpose, perhaps even a higher purpose, but one must keep in mind that there is a world of difference between church world and corporate realm.

Have you ever wondered what Jesus' own mission statement might have looked like? I believe he actually states it

---

16 John 10:10 (NAB).
17 John 10:10 (TLB).
18 *The Purpose Driven Life: What on Earth am I Here For?* by Rick Warren (2002).

quite concisely in John 10:10, an easy reference to remember. Unfortunately, a goodly number of Bible versions seriously miss the mark with their translation of one key word. The original Greek adverb *perisson*, means *superabundantly, over and above*, the equivalent of a grade of A^+. The Latin Vulgate translates the Greek original accurately by using the comparative adverb *abundantius*, more abundantly. The *more abundant life, life in all its fullness*, that's what Jesus was talking about. That was his mission statement: to bring more abundant life. All of his teaching, preaching, healing, and whatever else fits perfectly under one purpose: to bring about *more abundant life*.

For a moment, join me in an imagery exercise. Imagine the concept of one's *spiritual life* being spread out over a continuous spectrum. At one end is *more abundant life*, while at the other, *barely existent life*. Peter and Paul each experienced a radical, life-altering event which propelled them almost overnight from wherever they happened to be on that continuum toward *more abundant life*. But such drama is the exception not the rule in spiritual life. Most of us just plod along, inching our way along that continuum, eventually winding up somewhere in between.

At times I will make some wrong choices and move away from *more abundant life;* and sometimes by God's grace and inspiration I'll move toward it. For the most part, my quest for the *more abundant life* can only be attained by degrees, by holy persistence, and by spiritual exercise. At first, I may somehow *hear* about the concept of a more abundant life. Gradually, as my interest peaks, I may *listen* more intently. I may first *observe* a clearly more abundant life in another, but only later after taking a closer *look* and focusing more intently do I begin to realize what's going on. As Christ-followers, that's what spiritual development is all about. We progress in stages; we inch our way by degrees toward what

Teilhard de Chardin called the *Omega Point*.[19]

In seeking the more abundant life, I must at all costs avoid becoming a *Christ-skeptic*, that stiff-necked posture typically exhibited by neo-Pharisees whose hearts are hardened,[20] whose minds are closed, and who have all but denied any possibility of supernatural life. Sometimes a cheap substitute for the apparently superabundant is mistaken for the real thing.

> They have mouths, but they cannot speak;
> Eyes have they, but they cannot see;
>
> They have ears, but they cannot hear;
> noses, but they cannot smell;
>
> They have hands, but they cannot feel;
> feet, but they cannot walk;
> they make no sound with their throat.
>
> Those who make them are like them,
> and so are all who put their trust in them.[21]

The prophet Ezekiel expressed similar sentiments:

> The word of the Lord came to me: "Son of man, you dwell in the midst of a rebellious house, who have eyes to see, but see not, who have ears to hear, but hear not; for they are a rebellious house. Therefore, son of man, prepare for yourself an exile's baggage, and go into exile by day in their sight; you shall go like an exile from your place to another

---

19 A term coined by French Jesuit Pierre Teilhard de Chardin (1881–1955), who argued that the Omega Point was the Logos or Christ. Being both Alpha and Omega, beginning and end, Jesus was gradually drawing all things, including us, to himself.

20 Psalm 95:8 Harden not your hearts (*Nolite obdurare corda vestra*).

21 Psalm 115:5-8.

place in their sight. Perhaps they will understand, though they are a rebellious house.²²

Every Sunday evening in the seminary we would chant these words from Psalm 115, a sad but true depiction of idols and their artisans. What a pity. Sculptures designed with all those senses which can never be used. So beautifully carved, so wonderfully molded, so exquisitely fashioned, yet so functionally useless. When Jesus taught on *abundance*, he was talking about my spiritual life not my real estate assets. Some televangelists unfortunately have perverted that teaching, promising riches as a reward for virtue. That totally misses the point. Such a reading is both wrongheaded and misleading. Following that brand of theology, if the dollars don't roll in, then the extent of one's faith is called into question. Jesus clearly commented on mammon.²³ He said essentially that it's an either/or proposition: I cannot connect wealth and faith. Neither one proceeds from the other.

---

22 Ezekiel 12:1-16.
23 Matthew 6:24 "No man can serve two masters: for either he will hate the one, and love the other; or else he will hold to the one, and despise the other. Ye cannot serve God and mammon." (KJV).

ACCESSIBILITY

There once was a bishop from Boston
Whom letters and phone calls were lost on;
You could make a great fuss
Even take the next bus,
But you wouldn't get in to see Lauston!

Well, once upon a time I did have a bishop with whom it was rather difficult to get an appointment. No, it wasn't in Boston nor was his name *Lauston*, but it helps to change names and places when trying to craft a limerick! The bishop's executive secretary, well, let's call her Jill. Some priests in that diocese had adapted a well-known scripture to express their frustration. The original text says:

> No one comes to the Father
> except through me.[24]

But their new, revised, non-standard version goes:

> No one comes to the Father
> except through Jill!

Well, poor Jill was just doing her best to keep things on track as the bishop wanted, isolated in his own episcopal bubble and sequestered from potentially "troublesome" priests. Well, so much for our bishop-in-hiding and the

---
24 John 14:6.

priests' comedic turn-of-phrase. But what about that original scripture? What did Jesus actually say? More importantly, what did he mean? What was the entire context of that verse?

> Jesus said to [Thomas], "I am the way, and the truth, and the life. No one comes to the Father except through me.

What did that mean in the *mind* and *heart* of Jesus? And what didn't it mean? On the surface, the English and original Greek wording of that verse seem pretty straightforward. But not really. There's a great deal more to it. The first verse of that chapter provides further essential context:

> Do not let your hearts be troubled. Believe in God, believe also in me. In my Father's house there are many dwelling places [mansions, KJV]. If it were not so, would I have told you that I go to prepare a place for you?[25]

This passage serves as one of the several options for the Gospel at a Requiem Mass. Choosing this passage makes sense, for example, if the deceased person hadn't been in church for years, belongs to another faith tradition, or maybe might even have self-identified as an agnostic. The hymn "There's a Wideness in God's Mercy"[26] counterbalances the apparent harshness of the scripture that *no one comes to the Father except through me*. If humankind could only grasp the wideness, latitude, liberality, and total optimism of God! With God, one size never fits all. Everyone is unique. God doesn't manufacture duplicates. When our earthly sojourn is past, our Creator wants all of us—whoever we are and

---

25 John 14:1.
26 *Hymnal 1982*, "There's a Wideness in God's Mercy" by Frederick William Faber (1814-1863) #469, 470.

wherever we happen to be on life's journey—to come home.

The *dwelling places* (I prefer the KJV translation *mansions*) are *many* because each of us is unique. Each has pursued a different path in a unique way. And so, it would follow divine logic that we each have unique quarters waiting for us in the *Life after Life*.[27] And to the surprise of some, those suites have no hangtags reading RESERVED FOR CHRISTIANS ONLY. Everybody gets a room. That's the way it has to be. Heaven is *inclusive* not *exclusive*. But how is this possible? Doesn't God have some version of an executive secretary to keep him in a celestial bubble and pesky people away? Especially those who refuse to tow the party line? After all, just how accessible *is* God? What did Jesus mean when he said "No one comes to the Father except through me?" Are only practicing, card-carrying, tithe-paying Christians in good standing invited? My answer is a resounding *no*.

If no one can come to the Father, God the Creator, without first going through the Son, Jesus Christ, then what about the rest of humanity? What will happen to Jews, Buddhists, Muslims, atheists, agnostics, and everyone else? Do they also get lodging? Or are they doomed to be eternally homeless? Is this a *deja vu* experience of what the Holy Family heard on Christmas Eve, "Sorry, no room at the inn?" In my view, the answer is simple yet subtle. You see, I believe anyone can come to God through Jesus either *explicitly* or *implicitly*. How does this work? Practicing Christians come through the explicit belief that Jesus Christ is the Son of God and therefore acknowledged as their Lord and Savior. But others are likewise able to come to God through Jesus, but this happens *implicitly* rather than *explicitly*.

For any number of possible reasons, some people have not received the gift of faith. But in the larger scheme of

---

27 See Raymond A. Moody, *Life after Life* (1975).

things, as far as God is concerned, that's not a deal-breaker. Ultimately, all our Creator asks is that we've tried to do our best, given the hand we've been dealt. I believe that's all God really *does* ask. God is love. And God loves each and every individual, whether card-carrying churchgoers or just people trying to live out the Golden Rule. Some people will tell you that humankind neatly divides into Christians and everybody else. That simplistic view is roundly contradicted by a book entitled *Your God Is Too Small*.[28] Those convinced of such a narrow-minded reading of that scripture would do well to hear the hymn "There's a Wideness in God's Mercy." God welcomes everybody. God invites all to come dine with him. There's more than enough for me and everybody else. When I think about what heaven might look like, I see a sign posted outside a fine dining restaurant which says NO WAITING.

Fortunately, God has no "Jill," no executive secretary, no actual gatekeeper, not even the legendary doorman, St. Peter. God is no bishop-in-a-bubble, but our *Emmanuel*, God with us, God for us, and that means, for all of us. So, let's invite one another. See you at the heavenly banquet! You know, that's the dinner party that begins right here, right now, on earth.

---

28 J.B. Phillips, *Your God is Too Small* (1953).

Adolescence

Recently I watched a superb documentary, from beginning to end, on the Second World War. I got disgusted all over again at the human carnage, the wanton waste, and the barrage of images conveying once again "man's inhumanity to man." Sadly, not long ago, history seems to have repeated itself in the Ukraine. I was stunned all over again to witness how one insane demagogue can corrupt his fellow citizens and destroy innocent people and all their belongings with such a toxic agenda.

What happened in Germany during the 1930's was the proverbial perfect storm. The German populace, massively dissatisfied with their lot in life after the failed debacle of the First World War, yearned for a messiah who could finally lead them out of misery into prosperity. They proved an easy mark for the self-proclaimed *Fuehrer* who blamed Jews, Catholics, homosexuals, artists, liberals, and every other non-blond, non-blue-eyed, non-Aryan for their postwar plight. He promised to lead them out of all that. That resulted in Europe, Japan, the Philippines, and Pearl Harbor all being turned into hateful, catastrophic death zones. More than sixty million perished including six million Jews. War is madness and hatefulness, but when you add bigotry and greed into the mix you have a living hell.

Only God knows how different our world might be today, had those sixty million souls been allowed to go on living. Our Hebrew Lord no doubt wept bitter tears over the execution of his fellow Jews at the order of one crazed bigot. Hitler promised that Germans would eventually reign as the master race. Instead, his diabolical demagoguery caused Germans to be despised for decades. Silence can be golden, but silence is nothing but fools' gold when wanton inhumanity goes unchecked.

But can we speak about silence in a larger, more generous context? When can silence truly be golden, as the proverb suggests? What environment allows us to experience a happier, holier *sanctuary of silence*? Silence is golden when we give God space to speak and for us to listen.

In senior year of high school, all were required to make a traditional silent retreat. Each homeroom went away for a weekend to a Jesuit Retreat House. For me, that retreat was about trying to discern my future. Was God calling me to become a Roman Catholic priest or to get married and engage in some other profession? The retreat master only told me "I could see you in either scenario." Little did that priest know what God actually would have in store for me.

The retreat house chapel fascinated me. Octagonal in design, the altar stood right in the center with pews surrounding it. What dazzled me more than the architecture was the inscription carved on the face of the altar, ADULESCENS, TIBI DICO SURGE![29] Jesus had said these words as he healed a centurion's servant. Whoever selected that inscription must have had the adolescents in mind who would be coming there on retreat.

Can one trace any relationship between preserving love amidst inhumane treatment and finding oneself contemplating the crossroads of life? I think that there is and that it very much has to do with the words of that stunning altar inscription. Both refer to resurrection life, to a holy and

---

29   Luke 7:14 "Young man, I say to thee, arise!"

wholesome *rising up*, rather than the opposite: the unholy, toxic *uprising* advocated by the false prophets in human history. Jesus addresses the centurion's servant as *adulescens*, like English *adolescent*, a term which applies to young men as well as women. It addresses all the "young." How come that altar inscription made such an impression on me? Because *adulescens* does not simply refer to youngsters but to anyone who is *in the process of becoming an adult,* growing up:

> until all of us come to the unity of the faith and of the knowledge of the Son of God, to maturity, to the measure of the full stature of Christ.[30]

Whether graduating senior or senior citizen, we're all supposed to be continuing to grow up into the *full stature of Christ*. Called to rise up from the earth as does a flower or plant, we are expected to embrace a lifelong pursuit of growing into *maturity, to the measure of the full stature of Christ*. The challenge of moving out of *adolescence* begins with a ceremony often called *graduation*, a word derived from Latin *gradus*, or step. It's about taking the next step in life. But the word *commencement* is a better word choice than *graduation* because it's all about new beginnings rather than old endings.

The author Eugene Peterson translates a passage from Ephesians which speaks in modern idiom to the phenomenon of adolescence. He says:

> No prolonged infancies among us, please. We'll not tolerate babes in the woods, small children who are an easy mark for imposters. God wants us to grow up, to know the whole truth and tell it in love—like Christ in everything.[31]

---

30 Ephesians 4:13.
31 Ephesians 4:14-15 (MSG).

Senior retreat didn't give me any easy answers to a life decision. Thankfully, the retreat master wouldn't do my spiritual homework for me. He told me I needed to listen to Jesus over that weekend amidst the sounds of silence in such sacred space. And no matter what our biological age or vocational station in life, Jesus extends the same invitation to all of us: *Adulescens, tibi dico surge!* Wherever we are in trying to grow into the full stature of Christ, Jesus invites us to get up from our lethargy and get on with listening to whatever God might in store for us.

May each of us be inspired do just that, get up and get on with the unfolding discernment of life in the Spirit. Nobody else, no outside expert or consultant can do our homework for us. It's our own personal quest for the *more abundant life*.[32]

---

[32] John 10:10.

ANXIETY

Have you ever wondered why spell-check corrected one of your words, and not because you misspelled it? That word-processing feature can be either bane or blessing. "I am *anxious* to see you" gets corrected to "I am *eager* to see you." But, wait a minute, I said *anxious*, not *eager*! No matter. Spell-check always knows better, right? Why auto-correct my word choice? One particular collect gave me pause to think about just that:

> Grant us, Lord, not to be anxious about earthly things, but to love things heavenly; and even now, while we are placed among things that are passing away, to hold fast to those that shall endure.[33]

From this prayer, one could construct an equation of proportionality:

$$\frac{\text{earthly anxieties}}{\text{heavenly love}} \quad \frac{\text{concern}}{\text{concerns}} \quad \frac{\text{things passing away}}{\text{things that endure}}$$

Earthly anxieties are to *heavenly love*, what *things that are passing away* are to *things that endure*. Or put another way: *earthly anxieties* relate to *things that are passing away*, things that are only temporary; whereas *heavenly love* is associated

---

[33] *Book of Common Prayer (BCP 1979)* Prayer Book of the Episcopal Church (TEC), Proper 20, p. 234.

with *things that endure*, things of lasting permanence.

But in and of itself, is *anxious* a *bad* word? Rabbi Edwin H. Friedman in his best-known work, defined a well-differentiated leader as:

> someone who has clarity about his or her own life goals, and, therefore, someone who is less likely to become lost in the anxious emotional processes swirling about.... and therefore, can maintain a modifying, non-anxious, and sometimes challenging presence....[34]

The word *anxious* is a close cousin of the German word *Angst*, even borrowed into English as *angst* which derives from German *eng*, meaning *narrow* or *constricted*. Spellcheck, you see, is trying to do a good deed: to steer us away from any sense of narrow, fearful containment, and point us toward hopeful anticipation. Better to be *eager* than *anxious*. But *are* we more often eager or more often anxious?

Richard Rohr talks a lot about the first and second halves of life.[35] The first half is all about climbing the so-called ladder of success, about getting to the top of our game—whatever that might be—and the whole process of acquiring more and more "stuff." It's all the *stuff* we wind up having to unload in the second half of life, whether that be material goods or unhealthy spiritual habits. The trouble with the ladder, as Thomas Merton points out, is that we may spend our whole life climbing what we consider a ladder of success, only to discover that once we arrive at the top, our ladder is leaning against the wrong wall! What an unsettling concept! We're so anxious to start climbing, we don't even bother to take stock of where we're headed. Sad, but often too true. Pope

---

34 *Generation to Generation* (1985).
35 See Richard Rohr, *Falling Upward* (San Francisco, CA: Jossey-Bass, 2011).

St. Leo the Great once said in one of his sermons that "the business of this life should not preoccupy us with its anxiety and pride."[36] Perhaps we might rephrase that to the *busyness* of this life. So often what we are doing is simply spinning our wheels and getting nowhere fast.

Friedman's observation about how we "become lost in the anxious emotional processes swirling about" is often our main preoccupation during the first half of life. Are we not sometimes "tossed to and fro, and carried about with every wind of doctrine?"[37] Overstimulated, do we not often find ourselves on emotional overload, unable to find our center and embrace peace? Instead, we are prone to climb just one more rung, trying to escape the rat race. But unfortunately, that seldom happens.

Rohr tells us we need to graduate as soon as possible from the pitfalls of permanent residence in the first half of life to the second. And rest assured, this isn't about any arbitrary, symmetrical division between birth and age fifty. Unfortunately, it's not that simple. Our essential task is to exit as safely as possible the *first half* of life, one often fraught with earthly anxieties, to make that period as brief as possible. Instead of getting stuck there, it is important that we fashion a *container* whose sole purpose is housing our *spiritual life*, that *heavenly thing* that will last forever. Returning to our proportion, we find something like this:

earthly anxieties	concern	things passing away
heavenly love	concerns	things that endure

We can see that *anxiety*, the outward manifestation of inner *fear*, needs to be wholly supplanted by love. In one of

---

36 See the *Patrologium Latinum* 54, 366-367: Sermon #15, "On the Lord's Passion", 3-4.
37 Ephesians 4:14.

his many writings, Henri Nouwen said this:

> "We are a fearful people. The more people I come to know and the more I come to know people, the more I am overwhelmed by the negative power of fear. It often seems that fear has invaded every part of our being to such a degree that we no longer know what a life without fear would feel like. We live in a house of fear and it often becomes a prison for us."[38]

The Letter of James details practically every behavior that leads to *fearful anxiety*:[39]

- Climbing for upward mobility
- Striving for self-promotion
- Craving things at any price
- Selfish ambition
- The end justifying the means
- Coveting what we can never realistically have, which breeds discontent, disputes, conflicts
- Carnal appetites run amok
- "Gimme" prayers that never succeed in getting the results we want
- Hanging on to things that need to pass away
- Wisdom that is clearly "not from above"

Wow. What a litany of horrors! In other words, James agrees with Rohr. If we try to hold on to the developmental first half of life stage, we sign on for the perils suggested by that long litany of horrors. Well, if that list breeds *earthly anxieties*, then what, pray tell, would breed *heavenly love*? The imagery of the psalms paints pictures of people who delight in the Lord, who think about God constantly:

---

38 *Lifesigns: Intimacy, Fecundity, and Ecstasy in Christian Perspective* (1989).
39 See James 3:13—4:8.

> They are like trees
> planted by streams of water,
> bearing fruit in due season,
> with leaves that do not wither;
> everything they do shall prosper.[40]

In a magnificent valley on the island of Oahu in Hawaii, a beautiful stream runs through the property of a certain retreat house. The stream bed with its flowing water rushing down out of the mountains was my all-time favorite meditation spot. The plants and trees in and around that stream were absolutely verdant, full of life. Not a withered leaf nor decayed branch in sight. A vivid picture of what life is like when nourished by Living Waters![41]

Those who graduate to the second half of life find heavenly *love* instead of *earthly anxieties*, *living water* instead of *stagnant pools*. We read in John's Gospel:

> Jesus cried out, "If anyone thirsts, let him
> come to me and drink. Rivers of living
> water will brim and spill out of the depths
> of anyone who believes in me this way,
> just as the Scripture says."[42]

One need look no further than Proverbs 31 to find yet another secret for success, a key to discovering the positive qualities promised for the second half of life. This oft-quoted passage describes the perfect spouse, first and foremost *self-giving*, rather than *self-seeking*.

---

40 Psalm 1:3.
41 John 7:38 Let the one who believes in me drink. As the scripture has said, 'Out of the believer's heart shall flow rivers of living water.'
42 John 7:38 (MSG).

> She looks well to the ways of her
> household, and does not eat the bread of
> idleness.[43]

Such a spouse is interested solely in the welfare of the family, without an ounce of selfish ambition to be found anywhere. Gratified, even buoyed up, by the love within her household, such a spouse is, as Ignatius Loyola put it, "a [person] for others." Her lifelong partner prudently and fearlessly proclaims:

> Many women have done excellently,
> but you surpass them all."
>
> Charm is deceitful, and beauty is vain,
> but a woman who fears the LORD
> is to be praised.[44]

And for that matter, any *person* who fears the Lord fits that description. Any man, woman or child who, reverencing God makes that conscious choice to move out of the *House of Fear* into the *House of Love*, is destined to enjoy the heavenly refreshment of *Living Waters*.

Will it be *anxious* or *eager*? Which word is your choice?

---

43 Proverbs 31:27.
44 Proverbs 31:29-30.

Appearance

The word *appearance* is popular around Hollywood. Such-and-such an A-lister is about to *appear* in the next blockbuster film or series on Hulu or Netflix. Or we hear that some lesser luminary was just featured in a new stage production where they had a *cameo appearance*. A *special guest appearance* by any actor generally tends to pique our curiosity as well. All these *appearances* are widely publicized to stimulate our interest. Didn't somebody say, "It pays to advertise?" But then there's one particular *appearance*, a coming attraction, though well-advertised many times over in the Hebrew Bible, that didn't draw that much of an audience. Yet it drew a significant audience.

Outside of his parents, those witnessing the *appearance* of the Babe of Bethlehem formed a highly unlikely audience. Gathered at the stable were farm animals and strangers. The human audience consisted of three men who followed a star, wherever it led. The animals were there anyway, it was a barn. Remember the sign outside the front door of the inn? It was flashing NO VACANCY. The travelers who made up the audience are identified as *Magi*, denoting educated people of royal or high station. They were *astrologers*, but not soothsayers, fortune tellers or horoscope writers. That term *astrologer* referred to what we'd call a university-level research *astronomer*. These scholars were sufficiently curious to follow a hunch, a clue. They embarked on a research trip to see if what had been foretold would actually take place. These innocent, well-intentioned, and unsuspecting academics were unaware of Herod's hidden agenda. As men of the academy, they were simply traveling towards truth, moving towards the light. Their intellectual curiosity motivated them to embrace scientific method: research, find, verify, and then, when persuaded by the data, embrace the truth. And they would spare no effort in doing so, including embarking on a long and arduous trip guided only by celestial—and we might qualify—divine navigation.

This was the first Epiphany, the debut of the *new light of God's Incarnate Word*, a quite unconventional performance. No impressive, upscale venue this, but rather a freezing, harsh, outdoor event *in the bleak midwinter*. The only warmth available was provided by the breath of animals. And that's not all. There was yet one more curious inconsistency about this event. The visitors were *Gentiles*, not *Jews*. The Christ Child, *Yeshua ha-Mashiach*,[45] had none of his Chosen People for an audience. Ironically, Jesus' first appearance was not to those he was sent to redeem. Besides Mary and Joseph, he first appeared to a curious blend of dumb animals and highly educated Gentiles. From his infancy, Jesus began associating with the unlikely, the unpredictable, even the smelly. Who would ever have imagined that the long-awaited Savior would enter the world in such an undignified manner? Seen from a purely *human* perspective one would have to say that's absolutely upside-down and inside-out. But viewed from the *divine* perspective, it was absolutely spot on and as God intended.

The *Epiphany* event was also significantly different for another reason. This encounter between God and humankind was an *immanent* encounter. God, in the infant Jesus, was now up close and personal, rather than distant and dis-

---

45 Hebrew for "Jesus the Messiah."

engaged. The Magi, Gentiles not Jews, were now face-to-face with rather than distant from God. God would no longer seem unreachable and aloof, but present and in touch. Their *engagement* with divinity no longer remained exclusively *transcendent*, God being distant and unreachable, out there or up there somewhere else. From now on, God would prefer to appear as *Emmanuel*, God-with-us, rather than God-as-far-away-as-possible from us. How typical of Jesus to first reveal himself to the least likely, to outsiders, foreigners, even farm animals, rather than first appear to the so-called chosen people. How and to whom Jesus would first show himself prefigures his generous outreach to one and all. There would be neither outcasts nor the privileged. Things played out pretty much as John had reported:

> He came into the very world he created, but the world didn't recognize him. He came to his own people, and even they rejected him. But to all who believed him and accepted him, he gave the right to become children of God.[46]

The Feast of the Epiphany prefigures Jesus' open-door policy. He would be open to all creation, to all women and men, regardless of their credentials or lack thereof. The three gentlemen who visited Bethlehem are reported to have brought gifts. Caspar, Melchior, and Balthazar, figures from tradition rather than scripture, brought with them gold, frankincense, and myrrh, each gift loaded with symbolic meaning. The *gold* stands for the *royal* Christ, the King of Kings and Lord of Lords. The *frankincense*, a costly blend of aromatic spices, honors Christ as the Great High *priest*, acknowledging Christ as Deity, Godhead, and the One to whom incense

---

46 John 1:10-12 (NLT).

should arise.⁴⁷ And finally, they brought him *myrrh*, honoring Jesus as *prophet*, one who courageously speaks the mind of God. But myrrh also served as the traditional ceremonial burial spice. This gift likewise prefigured that Jesus too would be anointed with it, suffering every prophet's ultimate doom, cruel execution. And so, the three highly symbolic gifts of the Magi honored Jesus as prophet, priest, and king, so beautifully expressed in the opening words of the canticle entitled "A Song to the Lamb:"⁴⁸

> Splendor and honor and kingly power
> are yours by right, O Lord our God.
>
> For you created everything that is,
> and by your will they were created
> and have their being;

Both the exotic visit of the Magi as well as the kingly role Jesus Christ was destined to play in salvation history are foretold in Hebrew scripture:

> Nations shall come to your light, and
> kings to the brightness of your dawn.
>
> Lift up your eyes and look around; they
> all gather together, they come to you;
> your sons shall come from far away, and
> your daughters shall be carried on their
> nurses' arms.
>
> Then you shall see and be radiant; your
> heart shall thrill and rejoice, because the
> abundance of the sea shall be brought to
> you, the wealth of the nations shall come
> to you.

---

47 Psalm 141:2 "Let my prayer be counted as incense before you, and the lifting up of my hands as an evening sacrifice."
48 *BCP 1979*, Canticle 18, Revelation 4:11.

> A multitude of camels shall cover you, the young camels of Midian and Ephah; all those from Sheba shall come. They shall bring gold and frankincense, and shall proclaim the praise of the Lord.[49]

The very same prophecy is echoed in the Psalms:

> The kings of Tarshish and of the isles
> shall pay tribute,
> and the kings of Arabia and Saba
> offer gifts.
>
> All kings shall bow down before him,
> and all the nations do him service.[50]

Well before Paul would declare himself "apostle to the Gentiles," the Magi had arrived to be the very first Gentiles to welcome Christ:

> Although I am the very least of all the saints, this grace was given to me to bring to the Gentiles the news of the boundless riches of Christ, and to make everyone see what is the plan of the mystery hidden for ages in God who created all things...[51]

Jesus' first appearance in the drama of salvation history was no cameo appearance. It was *the* Epiphany, the reveal of all time. Once Jesus had shown his sacred face to our suffering humanity, he would never turn away, never abandon us, turn

---

49 Isaiah 60:3-6.
50 Psalm 72:10-11.
51 Ephesians 3:8-9.

a deaf ear, or leave us comfortless. That Christ had become enfleshed meant we'd never be without the *immanent* God, Emmanuel-within-us. It is significant that of all three costly gifts the Magi brought, our Savior kept only the *myrrh*, his burial spice. The *gold* he gave away to the poor and needy, and the *frankincense* he let ascend in praise of all humanity, rather than in praise of himself. He would embrace the life of a servant-leader, one who gives everything away and holds nothing back. Jesus' ultimate goal was justice, never greed; ever peace, never war.

Asking

You've probably seen or at least heard of that much beloved, quite long-running TV game show called *Jeopardy*. Hosting that show from 1984 to 2020 was the apparently ageless, professorial-looking host, Alex Trebek. On that show, at least, he never *asked* a single question. He just read off *answers* to questions from all sorts of cleverly-worded categories. Should a contestant not respond by asking a question, the dreaded buzzer would sound. To do so would have been wrong because contestants were *expected* to phrase their response as a question, not as an answer.

For example, take the category "Let the Games Begin." Trebek would read the following answer off his cue card: "A challenging TV game show running since 1984." The correctly-phrased response would be, "What is Jeopardy?" But if the contestant were simply to respond by saying "Jeopardy," you guessed it: the dreaded buzzer would sound.

The way this game show works is quite counter-intuitive. Wouldn't one expect a *quiz* show host to ask questions rather than give answers? But in order to win, a successful *Jeopardy* contestant is forced to think counter-intuitively.

In the First Book of Kings, we find the beloved story of Solomon interviewing *Yahweh*. Solomon, a man greatly devoted to worship, frequently offered sacrifice to God. His was an attitude of humility, devotion, and faithfulness. As their dialog began, God told Solomon he would grant whatever he asked for. How thrilled would we have been to get such an offer from God! Think about it. What might you have asked for? I'm afraid I'd be ashamed to confess the numerous things I'd ask for.

The Latin poet Juvenal, born about thirty years after the death of Jesus, was famous for his satires. His Tenth Satire, entitled "The Vanity of Human Wishes," is especially famous. In this 4,600-word document, Juvenal elaborates four frequent human wishes: the desire for riches, for power, for long life, and for good looks. As soon as he identifies a wish, he then proceeds to satirize, debunk, and utterly demolish it. He proves how vain and useless such wishes really are. In conclusion, the poet asks and answers a key question:

> Is there nothing then for which men shall pray? If you ask my counsel, you will leave it to the gods themselves to provide what is good for us. For in place of what is pleasing, they will give us what is best.

So, essentially Juvenal is saying, "Leave it to the gods." Translated into Judeo-Christian thought we might say, "Leave it to *Yahweh*" or "Leave it to the Lord."

Devout, humble, worshipful, and reverent Solomon, upon receiving his *carte blanche* from the Lord to ask for whatever he wanted, pauses for a brief moment, then simply asks for *the wisdom of discernment*. One of the psalms concludes by reminding us that:

> The fear of the Lord is the beginning of wisdom;
> those who act accordingly have a good understanding.[52]

And please, let us properly understand what is meant by

---

52 Psalm 111:10.

the word *fear* here: not that cowering, dread-filled, apprehensive fear, but rather an awesome, respectful reverence before the Lord. Such was exactly Solomon's stance. He would constantly approach worship with a deep sense of reverence, with awe, humility, and gratitude. His stance, disposition, and mindset would become God's window into his very soul!

Like St. Ignatius Loyola many centuries later, Solomon wanted to be a man for others, someone far more interested in helping others than helping himself. Solomon asked God:

> Give me, your servant, a discerning heart,
> so that I may distinguish good from evil
> and govern your people with wisdom.[53]

You see, Solomon asked the right question. He asked for *wisdom*, not riches, power, long life, or good looks. And quite predictably *Yahweh* responded quite generously. Rather than simply saying "right," God previewed a whole host of coming attractions, attested to much later in Matthew's Gospel:

> But seek ye first the kingdom of God, and
> His righteousness; and all these [other]
> things shall be added unto you.[54]

Solomon was to get a huge bonus:

> The Lord was pleased that Solomon
> had asked for this. So God said to him,
> "Since you have asked for this and not
> for long life or wealth for yourself, nor
> have asked for the death of your enemies,
> but for discernment in administering

---

53 1 Kings 3:9.
54 Matthew 6:33 (KJV).

> justice, I will do what you have asked. I will give you a wise and discerning heart, so that there will never have been anyone like you, nor will there ever be. Moreover, I will give you what you have not asked for—both wealth and honor — so that in your lifetime you will have no equal among kings. And if you walk in obedience to me and keep my decrees and commands as David your father did, I will give you a long life."[55]

Wow! What an unexpected windfall for Solomon. It was almost as if he had won at Double Jeopardy! Ephesians reinforces the same message. Paul is cautioning his fledgling community to be smart, to seek being filled *only* by the Holy Spirit and by no one or nothing else:

> So then, be very careful how you live. Don't live like foolish people but like wise people. Make the most of your opportunities because these are evil days. So don't be foolish, but understand what the Lord wants. Don't get drunk on wine, which leads to wild living. Instead, be filled with the Spirit.[56]

Well, there we have it. Solomon lived right. His heart was in the right place. He had an appropriate relationship with the Lord. He was ready both to hear and to listen. He stood in the line of David. When given the opportunity, Solomon asked for the right thing, and he did not waste that one wish. He simply asked for wisdom.

---

55 1 Kings 3:10-14.
56 Ephesians 5:15-18 (GW).

Traditionally, the Church has referred to "Seven Gifts of the Holy Spirit" which first show up in the prophet Isaiah:[57]

1. Wisdom
2. Understanding
3. Counsel
4. Power
5. Knowledge
6. Fear of the Lord
7. Delight in the fear of the Lord

Later, First Corinthians, identifies nine gifts of the Holy Spirit:[58]

1. Word of wisdom
2. Word of knowledge
3. Faith
4. Healings
5. Working of miracles
6. Prophecy
7. Discernment of spirits
8. Different tongues
9. Interpretation of tongues

Whether you look at the Old Testament or the New, you can't miss that the very *first* gift is wisdom. Solomon did choose well. What do we ask God for? What about us? If, given the opportunity to make one unrestricted wish, what would you or I ask for?

---

57 Isaiah 11:2-3.
58 1 Corinthians 12:7-11.

BAPTISM

Grant that all who are baptized into Jesus'
Name may keep the covenant they have
made, and boldly confess him as Lord and
Savior.[59]

Parish priests get some of the darndest phone calls. Terminology, vocabulary, and word choice have always fascinated me. How one expresses something reveals a lot. Admittedly, clergy can get somewhat cynical. Rather than being snarky, clergy should be grateful whenever someone makes a request of the church. One bank used to advertise itself as "the bank that says yes." I believe the church should do the same, at least most of the time.

It would be preferable, however, that people not use the church for "occasional services." Faith communities are intended to meet regularly rather than occasionally. It has been quipped that some people come to church only three times during their lifetime: "when they're hatched, matched, and dispatched." I don't think we should be cynical, least of all in the pulpit. One Christmas Eve a Silicon Valley priest dropped a bombshell as he greeted his standing-room-only crowd with "Well, it's so nice to see all the CEOs tonight." So far, all the many entrepreneurs present were beaming.

---

59   BCP 1979, p. 214 from the "Collect at the Baptism of the Lord."

They heard the priest patting them on the shoulder, but this was far from what he meant. He continued, "And of course by that I mean the 'Christmas-and-Easter-Onlys.'" Some chuckled, but others bristled never to darken the door of that church again, Christmas Eve or otherwise.

Well, there *is* a point to all this, but before we go, one more story. This one is a real doozie about Baptism. A grandparent once called up the parish priest announcing that she now had a new granddaughter and she'd like to bring her to church and "have her done." To which the somewhat jaded priest replied, "Madam, would that be medium-rare or well-done?" The caller obviously missed his warped irony, the conversation continued, and the baptismal service eventually took place.

The point of this story is that Baptism is not about getting someone or something *done* or checking off a to-do list. And a baptismal certificate is not a paid-up fire insurance policy. Baptism implies embracing a radical, permanent, life-altering state. When a child is brought for baptism, that implies the parents and sponsors are prepared to make a serious commitment—indeed a *vow*—to nurture the child's faith until adulthood. The Anglican, Roman Catholic, and Orthodox churches stand committed to the tradition of infant baptism. That being the case, when someone inquires about "having their baby done," that should serve as an outward and visible sign of that family's need for sacramental instruction.

That's what needs to be *done* and done right. And the Church does it right, when the responsible parties understand what's going on. They need to understand what they are promising to do on behalf of the child. Too often baptismal preparation is hasty, improvised, *pro forma*, and poorly *done*. Too often neither parents nor sponsors understand the sacrament. No wonder they so seldom follow through. Too often, as in this curious phone call, is a grandparent or some other relative metaphorically "driving the bus" to baptism. As Western culture has changed dramatically over time, so have attitudes toward matters religious. People today don't care about such things because societal values and lifestyles have shifted. And while fighting culture wars is a losing battle, the Church is still responsible to teach what Baptism is and is not.

So, aside from the candidate, what are the essentials for a valid baptism? Simply two: (1) ordinary water poured or sprinkled over candidates or immersing them; (2) while saying the words "I baptize you in the name of the Father, and of the Son, and of the Holy Spirit." That's all. The baptismal ritual may be embellished with hymns, prayers, anointing with chrism, Eucharist, and so on. All those are enhancements. The only two essentials are plain water and invoking the Trinity.

Baptism can be in a Methodist, Catholic, Presbyterian, Episcopal, Baptist or some community church, or in no church. All are *valid* Christian baptisms as long as the two essential conditions of the water and the words are met. And Baptism never needs to be repeated.

Some denominations, not considering Baptism an unrepeatable sacrament, insist a person baptized as an infant then undergo, as an adult, a *second* baptism by immersion. There is no such sacrament as a *second* baptism! If there is serious doubt whether a person had ever been baptized, the Church conducts a simple *conditional* baptism. There is *one faith, one Lord and one baptism.*[60] And strictly speaking, one is *baptized* a Christian, and only later *confirmed* for example as an Episcopalian, Methodist, Roman Catholic or Presbyterian.

---

60   Ephesians 4:5.

There are six key questions asked of a candidate at baptism. The first three *renounce* the world, the flesh and the devil. The second three *claim* Jesus Christ. Basically, three no's and three yesses. Visualize this from a compass perspective. Imagine someone facing 270 degrees or due West. Let us say that a compass reading of 270 degrees represents a completely unwholesome direction. In order to make a complete turn-around and face 90 degrees or due East, one would have to rotate 180 degrees. In baptism, one is promising to undertake that process, not an over-night operation but over time, indeed over a lifetime.

The grace of the sacrament of baptism equips one to turn away from the unwholesome, be it the world, the flesh or the devil, and face towards the wholesome. This involves a gradually turning, degree by degree, as we seek the face of Jesus. It might seem simple. But sacraments are not magic acts. They usually don't do their work instantaneously. But the grace of our conversion begins with the Sacrament of Baptism and is always there to draw on.

Baptism is the doorway to every other sacrament. But it is far more than a mere gateway or initiatory rite. Baptism is more accurately described as a *first ordination*. Baptism contains all the gifts of the Holy Spirit, including our empowerment for ministry, especially for lay diaconal service. In baptism we agree to "seek and serve Christ in all persons,"[61] especially the forgotten, the marginalized, and the invisible. A tall order, one might comment, yet the essence of a sacrament which seeks to turn us around 180 degrees from being sel*fish* to sel*fless*.

---

61   Baptismal Covenant, *BCP 1979*, p. 305.

BODY

A book recommended to me years ago was a brief history of the Church written by a monk of the Order of the Holy Cross.[62] The author borrowed the title from scripture.[63] A certain collect resonates well with the title:

> Give us grace, O Lord, to answer readily the call of our Savior Jesus Christ and to proclaim to all people the Good News of his salvation.[64]

Both corporately and individually belonging to the Body of Christ, we are personally invited to "answer readily the call of our Savior Jesus Christ and proclaim to all people the Good News of his salvation." We are not called to passive membership but to intentional action on behalf of the Body. We fulfill our corporate call by belonging to a faith community and our call to action by exercising whatever individual gifts we have been given. We might well ask ourselves just how we might accomplish such a daunting assignment. Recovery literature says it's "simple, but not easy." St. Paul the Apostle outlines for us the doctrine called the "Mystical Body of Christ,"[65] a core doctrine of Christian theology. Paul teaches how the various members of a human body would not imitate, envy, or bully another member

---

62 Bonnell Spencer, OHC, *Ye are the Body* (New York: Holy Cross Publications, 1965).
63 1 Corinthians 12:27.
64 *BCP 1979*, p. 215.
65 1 Corinthians 12:12-27.

because each has its own individual role to play for the good of the whole. And the parts of a human body don't go off and abandon their membership claiming "because I am not an eye, I do not belong to the body." Likewise, one member may not kick another out. The eye cannot say to the hand, "I have no need of you." In other words, all must remain, be active, and respect their co-members if the body is going to work. And no member may ever tell another to get lost.

Membership mandates *interdependence* not *independence*. Paul makes that crystal clear when he says that "God arranged the members in the body, each one of them, as he chose. If all were a single member, where would the body be?" The answer to that question is pretty obvious. There would be no body at all. When discussing a list of spiritual gifts, one naturally might wonder: is there any *hierarchy* among spiritual gifts?

To answer this question, one must properly understand the word *hierarchy*. The *hier-* has nothing to do with English *higher* but rather derives from Greek *hieros* meaning *sacred* or *holy*. *Hierarchy* literally means "that which begins with, originates in or has its source of authority from the holy or sacred."[66] Any ordering of spiritual gifts would therefore imply arranging them according to their holiness and wholesomeness for the Body. Any suggestion of their *rank* would necessarily have to do with how spiritually beneficial such gifts are for other members. How helpful, how healthful are my gifts for others in my own faith community, my family?

Applying these criteria, we could then agree there is a definite *hierarchy* among gifts shared within the Mystical Body which Paul prioritizes in descending order:

---

66 Greek: ἀρχή (beginning, origin, source of action) and ἱερός (sacred).

> first are apostles,
> second are prophets,
> third are teachers,
> then those who do miracles,
> those who have the gift of healing,
> those who can help others,
> those who have the gift of leadership,
> those who speak in unknown languages.

Paul concludes his list with some further rhetorical questions:

> Are we all apostles? Are we all prophets?
> Are we all teachers? Do we all have the
> power to do miracles?[67]

An obvious *no* to all four questions! Interestingly enough, Paul only chooses to assign numbers to his first three gifts, which in my view means that these as his top three. Our *first* call is to be *apostles*, to go forth to tell others about Jesus in general and about our family of faith in particular. Our *second* call is to be *prophets*, not *fortune teller*s or *prognosticators,* but simply called to "speak the truth in love,"[68] or as common parlance would have it, speak the truth to power. And our *third* call is to *teach*. No doctorate or teaching credential required! We simply share our faith in our own words, in our own way. We witness what the Mystical Body the Church means to us. That's quite credible enough. But should you still harbor doubts whether you simply lack *any* spiritual gifts to bring to the Church, just recall this familiar hymn:

> Come, labor on!
> Away with gloomy doubts and faithless fear!
> No arm so weak but may do service here:

---

67 1 Corinthians 12:29-30 (NLT).
68 Ephesians 4:15.

By feeblest agents may our God fulfill
His righteous will.[69]

No arm so weak but may do service here. Are you and I ready to come, labor on? Are we ready to claim the high calling angels cannot share? Are we ready to be the Body of Christ and individually members thereof? Are we ready to go forth, speak truth, and share faith? Are you and I ready to answer the call of our Savior Jesus Christ and proclaim to all people the Good News of his salvation? I believe we are—yes, right here, right now. May we be inspired to exit our comfort zone, and equipped to labor on, spread the Good News far and wide, Amen!

---

[69] *Hymnal 1982*, #541 "Come, Labor On."

BOOKENDS

> While he yet spake, behold, a bright cloud overshadowed them: and behold a voice out of the cloud, which said, "this is my beloved Son, in whom I am well pleased; hear ye him."[70]

These words are taken from Matthew's account of the Transfiguration. The Father's voice is heard in all three synoptic accounts recounting this event. God also pronounced these identical words at Jesus' Baptism:

> And the Holy Ghost descended in a bodily shape like a dove upon him, and a voice came from heaven, which said, "thou art my beloved Son; in thee I am well pleased."[71]

In the Episcopal liturgical year, Jesus' baptism is always celebrated the Sunday after the Epiphany.[72] The last Sunday after the Epiphany, at most, eight weeks later, likewise includes a Transfiguration Gospel.[73] What is significant about this? What relationship exists between Christmas and

---

70 Matthew 17:5 (KJV).
71 Here, Luke 3:22 (KJV). See also Matthew 3:17.
72 January 6th.
73 Matthew 17:1-9; Mark 9:2-9; Luke 9:28-36.

Epiphany? And why, at Christ's Transfiguration, does God the Father repeat verbatim what he had first proclaimed at Jesus' baptism?

Most scholars have lots of books and I'm no exception. I don't really need bookends because my bookshelves are crammed full. But people give you gifts. I treasure two pairs of bookends I got as gifts. Tidying up my study the other day, I ran across both sets which started me thinking about the function and purpose of bookends. They are *nice*, they can be decorative, even artistic, but are designed to hold relatively few books. If your shelves are crammed from one end to the other like mine, bookends become superfluous. They only get in the way. I use mine to hold about seven or eight books I consult regularly. Epiphanytide has a maximum of eight Sundays, and that's why *bookends* suggest some interesting symbolism.

I see Jesus' Baptism and Transfiguration as symbolic *liturgical bookends*, holding at most seven or eight Sundays between them. In what sense, then, do Matthew's words, "this is my beloved Son, in whom I am well pleased; hear ye him," heard at Jesus' Baptism and Transfiguration, qualify as liturgical bookends to Epiphanytide? Why are these words significant? They are *crucially* important because they are keys to understanding *identity* and *relationship*, namely who Jesus is and how we connect with him. The Sundays of Epiphany chronicle an evolving revelation of who Jesus is. To whom does he reveal himself? Epiphanytide begins at the manger where Jesus *first revealed his sacred face*.[74]

At his Baptism by his cousin John, a humble Jesus is revealed, one willing to self-identify as part of humankind. For Jesus to submit to baptism was quite ironic since, of all

---

74 *Hymnal 1982* #82 "Of the Father's Love Begotten" *And the Babe, the world's Redeemer, first revealed His sacred face.*

people, he would be the *only* one who never needed it. But he was willing to participate and model it for us anyway. Jesus' humble baptism prefigures his passion and death, when he would freely suffer and die *for us and for our salvation.*

Jesus' next appears at a wedding with his mother and first four disciples. His time, he reminded his mother, had not yet come. After mildly protesting, he obeyed Mary and performed his first miracle. At this wedding feast he not only blesses the future sacrament but also gives us a glimpse of his social side. Jesus loved people and loved to be generous. That would indicate why he didn't produce table wine but a rare costly vintage, and plenty of it. Here is some sacramental symbolism worth pondering.

We next encounter Jesus in the synagogue, duly observing the commandment, Remember thou keep holy the Sabbath Day. Invited to read the scripture lesson, Jesus deliberately chose Isaiah 61:1-2 requoted in Luke:

> The scroll of Isaiah the prophet was handed to him. He unrolled the scroll and found the place where this was written: "The Spirit of the Lord is upon me, for he has anointed me to bring Good News to the poor. He has sent me to proclaim that captives will be released, that the blind will see, that the oppressed will be set free, and that the time of the Lord's favor has come."[75]

The Jesus we encounter in this scene is a young man whose courage is mounting. He purposely picks a passage that not only clearly reveals his identity but likewise rattles many cages of the establishment:

---

[75] Luke 4:17-19.

> He rolled up the scroll, handed it back to the attendant, and sat down. All eyes in the synagogue looked at him intently. Then he began to speak to them. "The Scripture you've just heard has been fulfilled this very day!"[76]

For Jesus to state that "the Scripture you've just heard has been fulfilled this very day" was to throw down the gauntlet and declare, "I am the long-awaited Messiah. I am *Yeshua ha-Mashiach*, I am God's only Son, born for you and for your salvation." Jesus not only picked the exact text he wanted them to hear but to help them connect the dots he proceeded to spell out in no uncertain terms that *he* was chosen to put an end to business as usual. A new covenant between God and humankind had been born in the person of Jesus, which turned out to be more than his hearers could bear.

Sandwiched between the two beautiful bookends of Jesus' baptism and transfiguration, God's constant message is proclaimed over and over again: "This is my beloved Son, in whom I am well pleased; hear ye him." In the relatively short season of Epiphany, one with comparatively few books standing between two handsome bookends, we witness something remarkable, namely a developing profile in courage, as Jesus rises to the maturity of his vocation. And now, at the bookend on the right, *transfiguration*, he intentionally trudges up Mount Tabor with Peter, James, and John to prepare for the worst, because he needs quiet time with his Father. At the bookend on the left, *baptism*, we sense the energy and promise of what is to follow during the life of Christ. At the bookend on the right, transfiguration, we experience a different kind of energy, a mystical calm and

---

76 Luke 4:20-21.

centering moment. Here God's voice does not thunder as at his Baptism, but now speaks in that *still small voice*[77] "the peace of God which passeth all understanding."[78]

At this last crucial bookend, Peter is finally able to grasp the unique mission belonging to Jesus. This last epiphany depicts Jesus conversing with Moses and Elijah, with Jesus at the center, Moses and Elijah standing on either side of him. St. Augustine of Hippo comments:

> As soon as we hear these three mentioned together, we think of certain things for which they stand: Moses for the Law, Elias for the Prophets, Christ for the Gospel. As all three appear together on the Mount of Transfiguration, in full view of his disciples, Jesus' countenance and clothing began to shine as the sun. In this apparition, Jesus stood between Moses and Elias, thus reminding us that the Gospel bears testimony, as it were, on the one hand from the Law, and on the other from the Prophets.[79]

Moses and Elijah eventually fade within the cloud and then there stands *only Jesus*, internally transformed and externally transfigured, glowing with the radiance of his Father.

At this final bookend, Jesus must descend Mt Tabor to deal with the "real world," not unlike our own, a cruel, lonely, bruised, and hurting world. The Chosen People await the *Yeshua ha-Mashiach* promised in the Hebrew Scriptures. But the temple authorities cannot believe Jesus' words when he

---

77 1 Kings 19:12.
78 Philippians 4:7.
79 From a homily by St. Augustine of Hippo, Tract 17.

adds his commentary that "the Scripture you've just heard has been fulfilled this very day!" How could this kid be the real deal, they thought? He's just the carpenter's kid, a local, a laborer. What good can come out of that backwater village called Nazareth anyway? The so-called "Chosen People" would have to endure their own first Lent before anyone would be able to connect the dots and figure out that indeed Jesus was *ha-Mashiach*. Soldiers beneath his cross would realize it first:

> Now when the centurion, and they that were with him, watching Jesus, saw the earthquake, and those things that were done, they feared greatly, saying, truly this was the Son of God.[80]

Christmas and Epiphany eventually give way to Lent, a time of challenging spiritual work, the practice of prayer, penance, and preparation, providing us one more chance to reorient our direction in life. If, as the Gentile centurion belatedly realized, "truly this was the Son of God," then perhaps a consideration of the symbolic bookends of baptism and transfiguration might provide us the opportunity to invite God to help put our spiritual house in order. The well-known words heard every Ash Wednesday invite us to the Way of the Cross. "Remember that thou art dust, and to dust thou shalt return." Shall we make this walk together?

---

80 Matthew 27:54 (KJV).

Calling

The following notice was actually posted in a number of French churches:

> It is possible that on entering this church, you may hear the Call of God.
> On the other hand, it is not likely that he will contact you by phone.
> Thank you for turning off your phone.
> If you would like to talk to God, come in, choose a quiet place, and talk to him.
> If you would like to see him, send him a text while driving.

Posting such a notice on a church bulletin board certainly evokes laughter. But it serves to remind us that our God-connection is reciprocal, a two-way street. At times, God calls us; and at other times, we call God. More than any other church season, Christmas reminds us how God relates to us in two ways: (1) as *transcendent* or "totally other;" and (2) as *immanent,* meaning "residing within us." Rather than remain aloof from humankind, our Creator desired to come live among us and within us, which brings us back to the importance of Christmas. The Incarnation means that in sending his only Son, God made a choice between an *immanent* or *transcendent* presence. God preferred coming as *Emmanuel,* God within us. God did not opt to remain *transcendent,* remote as in the *Wizard of Oz.* God elected to be in touch rather than out of touch with humankind. If we view and indeed relate to God as exclusively *transcendent*, we fall woefully short of the divine will. God as *Emmanuel*[81] more closely resembles someone who checks regularly to see whether anyone's sent them a text message. In our reciprocal relationship with God, sometimes God leaves *us* a text, and at other times, we leave God one.

One particular prayer urges us to keep our mobile phone handy:

> Be gracious to all who have gone astray
> from your ways, and bring them again with
> penitent hearts and steadfast faith to embrace
> and hold fast the unchangeable truth of your
> Word.[82]

Here we are calling upon God to reach out to those who have strayed off the straight-and-narrow. At one time or another that would, of course, include you and me. We implore God to shower us with whatever grace necessary to take that call or read that text message and reply, entering into dialogue with our Lord. Lent extends an open invitation for God to return us once again to him in penitence and faith. We pray that we may be enabled to respond to the One who calls us. The message invites our prompt response to return the call. The message urges us to return to God now, sooner rather than later, and not procrastinate. Why *would* anyone put this opportunity off? At face value, it makes no sense to do so.

Well, during the Middle Ages, it became customary to delay baptism and therefore conversion of life[83] as late in life as possible. That way, in their younger years people could sow

---

81 Alternate spelling "Immanuel."
82 *BCP 1979*, p. 218, Collect for the Second Sunday in Lent.
83 What the "Rule of Benedict" 58:17 calls *conversatio morum*.

their wild oats *ad libidum* and then later on come to terms with God. Theirs was a far more *transcendent* relationship with God whom they considered distant, aloof, and out of touch with mortal humanity. Such a God, far away and unapproachable, would lack sufficient context to deal with the here and now, at least so they thought. Some would go as far as delaying baptism until their deathbed. Sacramentally speaking, since baptism wipes away all sin, original and actual, the later the baptism, the wilder the lifestyle one could get away with. An eleventh-hour baptism would absolve you of all your past peccadilloes and guarantee your nonstop flight heavenward. What a misguided theology! Who knows when their number is up?

Medieval monks passing one another along the cloister walk would exchange the somber greeting *memento mori*, remember death, rather than carefree words such as "eat, drink and be merry." The traditional Ash Wednesday formula, "Remember, mortal, that thou art dust, and unto dust thou shalt return" may ring as harsh as *memento mori* in some ears, but from both a physical as well as metaphysical standpoint, it still remains quite accurate. There is a scripture whose vivid imagery expresses the tender loving-kindness of God. Incontrovertibly, it sets the scene depicting how God prefers to relate to us: as *immanent* rather than as *transcendent*. In his frustration, Jesus cries out:

> O Jerusalem, Jerusalem, the city that kills the prophets and stones God's messengers! How often I have wanted to gather your children together as a hen protects her chicks beneath her wings, but you wouldn't let me.[84]

God-in-Jesus wants to shelter us under the protective,

---

84 Luke 13:34.

expansive wings of a mother hen symbolic of God's *motherly* caring for us. Earlier liturgical language refers exclusively to the *fatherly* goodness of God:

> And we earnestly desire thy fatherly goodness mercifully to accept this our sacrifice of praise and thanksgiving.[85]

The Lucan passage above, however, breaks new ground. Jesus stresses here God's *motherly goodness*. She spreads her wings as if to shelter us from the many storms of life, including the half-truths uttered by the Father of Lies. If we were to go look for a hymn about *God calling*, one by Will Thompson composed in 1880 would definitely fill the bill. Thompson's words and music were both inspired by the biblical scene where Jesus calls the blind man over who had been calling out to him:

> Many people scolded [the blind man] and told him to be quiet, but he shouted all the louder, "Son of David! Have pity on me!" Yeshua stopped and said, "Call him over!" They called to the blind man, "Courage! Get up! He's calling for you!" Throwing down his blanket, he jumped up and came over to Yeshua.[86]

Will Thompson's encouraging words[87] actually tie together two crucial realities, two sides of the same coin. God's call is on one side and our response is on the other. Like

---

85 *BCP 1979*, p. 335.
86 Mark 10:48-50 (CJB).
87 Thompson's best-known work is his classic, enduring gospel song "Softly and Tenderly Jesus Is Calling."

the proverbial *Hound of Heaven*,[88] God is neither passively available nor occasionally accessible to humankind but actively and assertively pursuing us, hounding us, imploring us repeatedly just as Will Thompson's refrain repeats after each stanza: *come home.*

> Softly and tenderly, Jesus is calling,
> Calling for you and for me;
> See, on the portals He's waiting and watching,
> Watching for you and for me. *Refrain.*
>
> Why should we tarry when Jesus is pleading,
> Pleading for you and for me?
> Why should we linger and heed not His mercies,
> Mercies for you and for me? *Refrain*
>
> Time is now fleeting, the moments are passing,
> Passing from you and from me;
> Shadows are gathering, deathbeds are coming,
> Coming for you and for me. *Refrain*
>
> Oh, for the wonderful love He has promised,
> Promised for you and for me!
> Though we have sinned, He has mercy and pardon,
> Pardon for you and for me. *Refrain*
>
> *Refrain*:
> Come home, come home,
> You who are weary, come home;
> Earnestly, tenderly, Jesus is calling,
> Calling, O children, "Come home!"

---

88 This 182-line poem was first published in the first volume of poems by Francis Joseph Thompson in 1893.

Changing

Can God change God's own mind? Can you and I change ours? Does God ever do such a thing, have a change of heart? How often do we or are we ever open to doing just that? One of the collects addresses God as the "author and giver of all good things" and asks that God *increase in us true religion.*

I once had a parishioner who, after hearing me preach about what I considered to be *true religion*, started whistling "Gimme that Old Time Religion" during coffee hour. I invited this fellow to meet me at a coffee bar later that week! After his second cup and our conversation on the topic of true religion, it was my fondest hope he might just begin to whistle a new tune. Serving as an interim at that parish rather than being the permanent pastor, I left for my next assignment without ever finding out whether he had changed his tune. From our brief, inconclusive discussion over coffee, it could certainly have gone either way. Maybe he did, maybe he didn't modify his view about what constituted *true religion*. He might have become even more firmly entrenched in his yearning for what he deemed *that old time religion*. Maybe he grew to despise even more any contemporary view of theology. Who knows? Saved by the bell, I got out of Dodge before ever finding out.

Don't you sometimes wonder whether God ever changes *God's* own mind? And what about Jesus during his earthly life? He was both God *and* man, right? And how about St. Paul? His mind, heart, and soul had all become dramatically changed. But was St. Paul ever able to change anyone else's mind? And if he did, how did he go about it? How effective *was* he?

The thirteenth-century Dominican theologian Thomas Aquinas posited five *attributes* that described God. Actually, these characteristics said more about what God is *not* than what God *is*. Essentially, Thomas taught that:

> **God is simple**, without composition of parts, such as body and soul, or matter and form.
>
> **God is perfect**, lacking nothing. God is distinguished from all other beings because God is completely self-contained. God has neither need for nor any interdependence upon other beings.
>
> **God is infinite**, that is, God is not limited in the ways that created beings are: physically, intellectually, or emotionally. God is limitless in all dimensions of being.
>
> **God is one**, that is, without diversification within God's self. We affirm that unity when in the Apostle's Creed we say I believe in one God.
>
> **God is immutable**, incapable of change or being changed as to God's essence or character, or in other words essentially unchangeable, immutable, and static.

Today, theology is far from such a simplistic, cut-and-dried assessment of God's nature. One of the most beautiful stories depicting the genuinely dynamic, fluid nature of God is illustrated in a passage from Jeremiah.[89]

In this story, the potter is God. The clay is God's human

---

89 Jeremiah 18:1-11.

creation. As he creates, the potter keeps his clay moist, fluid, and malleable. He does not allow it to get rigid or brittle. His options are wide open for whatever shape it might eventually take. He wants to work *with* the raw material. If it's not quite right, he *will* toss it back in with the rest of the clay, remold and rework it. He won't allow an imperfect product to rigidify and become brittle, lest someone simply toss it into the trash, shattering it into a thousand shards in some unfinished state of imperfection. And why? Because *God doesn't throw anything or anyone away.* God doesn't throw people away. God is the ultimate recycler, re-shaper, re-former, because God's world has no landfills. The Jeremiah piece attests that God doesn't discard us just because we're not yet perfect. He is willing to make the effort to cast and recast, mold and remold, all the while keeping the clay of creation moist and malleable, always giving us another chance, always waiting for you and me to reform, repent and turn our lives around in his direction.

And just as God can change God's own mind, God also gives us *repeated* opportunities to change ours and reconcile not only with God but with our fellow travelers as well.

Aquinas envisioned God as the perfect monolith. I prefer to visualize God as a gentle, patient potter, willing to work at molding and remolding, reworking the clay of our humanity "until all of us come to the unity of the faith and of the knowledge of the Son of God, to maturity, to the measure of the full stature of Christ."[90] Did not even Jesus himself change his mind during his encounters with people? Think of the woman whose daughter was ill and who persuaded him to change his position by reminding him that even dogs get to eat table scraps:

> [Jesus] answered [her], "It is not fair to take the children's food and throw it

---

90 Ephesians 4:13.

to the dogs." She said, "Yes, Lord, yet
even the dogs eat the crumbs that fall
from their masters' table." Then Jesus
answered her, "Woman, great is your
faith! Let it be done for you as you wish."
And her daughter was healed instantly.[91]

Change of mind, change of heart, change of soul—call it what you will. It all boils down to that Greek word metanoia (μετάνοια), that 180 degree turn-about. Changing is not as difficult as it might seem, especially when the right Potter is at the wheel. One venerable old renewal hymn sums it up well:

> You are the Potter, and I am the clay;
> You are Creator; craft me Your way;
> You are Designer, so I will stay
> Centered in the hollow of Your hand today.
>
> You are my Maker; You fashioned my frame;
> You know all about me; You call me by my name.
> Even the hairs on my head are numbered and known;
> You bottle ev'ry tear that falls as Your Own,
> As Your Own, Your Own.
>
> You are the Potter, and I am the clay;
> You are Creator; craft me Your way;
> You are Designer, so I will stay
> Centered in the hollow of Your hand today.[92]

---

91 Matthew 15:26-28.
92 "Have Thine own way, Lord" a hymn by Adelaide Addison Pollard, 1907.

DISCIPLINARIAN

> Now before faith came, we were imprisoned and guarded under the law until faith would be revealed. Therefore, the law was our disciplinarian until Christ came, so that we might be justified by faith. But now that faith has come, we are no longer subject to a disciplinarian.[93]

Years ago, Jesuit high schools and colleges had a rather unique faculty position, no longer found in those schools today. The position was called Dean of Discipline, and the Jesuit faculty member holding that position was referred to as "Father Dean of Discipline" in former days, always a priest. Some Jesuits were assigned duties other than teaching, only the better teachers holding classroom appointments. The rest were given other tasks, many not really requiring ordination, like that of a Bookstore Manager or a Dean of Discipline.

Believe it or not, if truth be told, I was pretty well-behaved in high school and college. No kidding! But I can't vouch for some of my classmates, especially in high school. Some would drive their cars onto campus at the last minute before the first bell and wind up having to park their jalopies on the grass. This was the kind of infraction which Father Dean of

---

[93] Galatians 3:23-25.

Discipline was not at all inclined to overlook. Parking on the grass infuriated him. He would roam about the parking lot like a raging lion seeking any illegally parked auto he might devour.[94] His penalty for each infraction was to let the air out of tires. One tire for a first offense, two tires for the next and so on. The tardy got the message. So did the Auto Club. As I said, being a "good boy," I always got to school early, so it never happened to me. But I always felt that kind of penalty was a bit extreme especially for a Jesuit. But after all, that was his job, to be the *disciplinarian*, and his rules were clear: "You park on my grass—you can call your own tow truck!"

These somewhat amusing trivia actually do relate to the topic. They outline the essential concept of a *disciplinarian*, translating the Greek word *paidagogos*, like our English *pedagogue*. A *paidagogos* was a *trainer of children*. The scripture cited at the beginning of this meditation said: *The law was our disciplinarian (trainer) until Christ came.*[95] Christ came to replace the *scaffolding* of the law, our *external* disciplinarian or trainer, with the gift of *faith*. Rather than simply responding in knee-jerk fashion to the letter of the law, our response is now made in the context of our faith.

There is so much rich theological content associated with the Christ event, it is a pity that the Christmas season is so short. Christmas needs to last much longer than twelve days.[96] Christ's Incarnation is so incredibly rich we need to keep the depth of that mystery before us daily. Christmas trees dry up, wreaths fall apart, ornaments get packed away, but *the miracle of Christmas* continues. What must human existence have been like before Christ came? How could

---

94 Adapted from 1 Peter 5:8. *Sobrii estote, et vigilate: quia adversarius vester diabolus tamquam leo rugiens circuit, quaerens quem devoret*, a scripture from "Compline," recited at day's end.
95 Galatians 3:24.
96 The twelfth day of Christmas is Epiphany, January 6th.

people ever have carried on without a redeemer? How were they able to get along with one another? What primitive operating system might they still have been stuck with?

In the third chapter of Galatians, Paul describes what life was like before Jesus' birth, pre-Incarnation life, before the Eternal Word became forever fused with the Babe of Bethlehem. He, for one, knew. We considered these words earlier. They bear repeating:

> Now before faith came, we were imprisoned and guarded under the law until faith would be revealed. Therefore, the law was our disciplinarian until Christ came, so that we might be justified by faith. But now that faith has come, we are no longer subject to a disciplinarian.[97]

A literal translation of the original would say, "we were guarded and shut up under the law."[98] That's pretty strong language and vivid imagery. It paints a picture of a prison where one is not only watched by armed guards but is literally *shut up, shut away, shut off,* and locked up in a cell. But that's exactly how Paul had experienced the human condition before Christ came: kept strictly under lock and key. The jailer was the *Law* or more precisely the 613 laws of Moses. Before Christ, every minute aspect of human behavior was rule-driven, law-governed, and fear-based. There simply *was* no alternative until Christ came. Christmas changed all that.

Paul begins by saying, "Before *faith* came." He then elaborates that *faith* came in the person of Jesus Christ. God had now provided *a new way.* God had thoroughly wiped our hard drive and installed a totally new *operating system.* And this system would not forever stagnate in a 1.0 version, but

---
97 Galatians 3:23-25.
98 Galatians 3:23.

over time would grow and develop just as the living organism of the Body of Christ. We would no longer be *law-driven* but *faith-inspired*, no longer *watched by jailers* but *watching for the Babe of Bethlehem*, who would come to free us. Jesus taught, lived, and demonstrated the new operating system for us: *spirit*, not law; *faith*, not law; *love*, not law. Now love would lead, love was in charge, and love must act. The operating manual had been rewritten. We obey the rules now because we love, not because we are afraid of being punished. Jesus never discarded the law. But he arranged it so that law would no longer lead in the dance of life, because love would. The new computer of life would run on love, not law.

> Do not think that I have come to abolish the Law or the Prophets; I have not come to abolish them but to fulfill them.[99]

Jesus fulfilled the law by putting love in the driver's seat. Keeping in mind that *discipline* is more related to *discipleship* rather than to *punishment*, the ultimate discipline is love. You and I are true *disciples* when we lead *disciplined* lives attuned to *love* rather than *fear*. We obey God not because we're *afraid* of God, but because we *love* God.

---

99 Matthew 5:17 (NIV).

DOUBT

Why ever would the Church, right after the glorious celebration Easter, choose to focus on the figure known as *Doubting Thomas*? *He is risen as he said,* right? Why now toss a wet blanket over it all, right? Well, there might be a very good reason why. Jesus' Resurrection calls an essential question: do I believe it or not? Throughout Hebrew scripture, humankind had to make similar choices: either doubt or believe. The last chapter of Matthew would qualify as a supporting scripture here:

> When they saw him, they worshiped him;
> but some doubted.[100]

Some will *always* doubt, won't they? Regardless about what, when, or where. Some people are just inveterate skeptics. There once was a popular game show called *Truth or Consequences*. Doubt also has its consequences. Every Advent we recall Zechariah's skepticism when he received the news that he was to become a father:

> Zechariah said to the angel, "How can I be sure this will happen? I'm an old man now, and my wife is also well along in years." Then the angel said, "I am Gabriel! I stand in the very presence of God. It was he who sent me to bring you this good

---

[100] Matthew 28:17.

news! But now, since you didn't believe what I said, you will be silent and unable to speak until the child is born. For my words will certainly be fulfilled at the proper time."[101]

"Since you didn't believe what I said," replied Gabriel, and Zechariah was silenced for his attitude. His tongue was loosened only months later at the dedication of his son in the temple. The first words Zechariah was able to form were those of the canticle now known as the *Benedictus*, traditionally prayed at Morning Prayer. Fast forward to the post-Resurrection event with the apostles gathered together. There we witness a much more strident attitude coming from Thomas. For some reason he'd been away when Jesus first appeared to his fellow disciples. So, when he finally did show up, the other disciples were incredibly eager to brief him on Jesus' visit and to share their joy. *We have seen the Lord*, they proclaimed.

> But [Thomas] replied, "I won't believe it unless I see the nail wounds in his hands, put my fingers into them, and place my hand into the wound in his side."[102]

His pesky response, patently more disrespectful than that of Zechariah, would likewise be challenged, but this time not by an angel. Jesus himself would appear and confront his disbelief:

> Eight days later the disciples were together again, and this time Thomas was with them. The doors were locked; but suddenly, as before, Jesus was standing

---
101 Luke 1:18-20 (NLT).
102 John 20:25 (NLT).

among them. "Peace be with you," he said. Then he said to Thomas, "Put your finger here, and look at my hands. Put your hand into the wound in my side. Don't be faithless any longer. Believe!"[103]

"Don't be faithless any longer. Believe!" Wow! How gently but firmly Jesus dealt with Thomas. One of my theology professors was trying to teach us about belief. He realized it would be next to impossible even for seminarians to assent to every tenet of the Nicene Creed right off the bat. He wanted us to approach each creedal statement prayerfully and honestly. His point which I'll never forget was this: "Remember: a thousand questions don't add up to a single doubt." That always stuck with me, because there's a genuine distinction between *doubting* something and *questioning* it. We need to know where we stand on any statement, creedal or otherwise. If we are unable to accept something right away, do we voice any questions we might have about it? Or do we just doubt and dismiss the whole thing out of hand?

When Gabriel announces to Mary that she was chosen to become the mother of Jesus, she would certainly have some reasonable *questions* about that revelation. But she asks about it without expressing outright *doubt*. The passage in Luke 1:28-38 reveals her yielded spirit. When the Archangel Gabriel appears out of nowhere, certainly she was much perplexed by his words and pondered what sort of greeting this might be. When he announced she was to become the mother of God, Mary questioned "How can this be, since I am a virgin?" Gabriel replied to this honest question by reminding Mary that "nothing will be impossible with God." Then Mary stated, "Here am I, the servant of the Lord; let it be with me according to your word." Zechariah and

---

103 John 20:26-27 (NLT).

Thomas, on the other hand, each in their own idiom reacted skeptically to the "breaking news." Certainly, Thomas reacted much more cynically than did Zechariah. But in contrast to both of them, Mary responded quite differently, in a gently inquiring way.[104] Those three biblical scenes each illustrate for us the difference between *doubting* and *questioning*. And they bear out my former professor's assertion that a thousand questions do not add up to a single doubt.

---

104 See "Lumen Gentium", 63-65: "As a new Eve she believed, not the serpent of old but the messenger of God, with a faith wholly free from doubt."

EMPTYING

I don't know about you, but before I buy a new book, some of the first things I look at are the publication date, table of contents, and the introductory chapter. I want to see where this book is coming from and where it's going. Is the topic current or outdated? Is it the latest edition? How often has this book been revised? Palm Sunday presents a kind of virtual book experience. Its title? *Holy Week*. And like most books, there's an *Introduction*, a *Table of Contents* and a *publication date*. All that information is on display Palm Sunday.

Our virtual book entitled *Holy Week* was published before the year 100 CE. The *Introduction* is recited when the palms are blessed. The traditional hymn "All Glory, Laud, and Honor" is then sung during a procession around the church, sometimes even out in public, around the block. Palms, pageantry, and pretty music make up the *Introduction* to our book entitled *Holy Week*. So far, so good.

But the ensuing chapters along with the rest of the *Table of Contents* are nothing like you might expect. It's not at all what you'd anticipate from such a spectacular, triumphal *Introduction*. The publication date? This book has no second edition. It hasn't been revised in over two thousand years. It remains a true first edition.

Palm Sunday sets off a chain of events, a process. As *Holy Week* unfolds, special attention is given to the Sacred Triduum of Maundy Thursday, Good Friday, and the

Saturday night Easter Vigil. Each commemoration highlights significant sacraments in the life of Christ.

On Maundy Thursday, Jesus demonstrates two sacramental moments. First, by washing his disciples' feet, he models the *diakonia* expected of apostles. They are to serve, not be served. Second, he will not leave his disciples comfortless, abandon them even for a moment, even as he prepares for execution tomorrow. He institutes the Eucharist, the Holy Communion by which he can remain with them—and us—until the end of time. When he says over the bread and the wine "This is my body; this is my blood" he means exactly what he says, even though his *real presence* is hidden under the appearances of bread and wine.[105]

On Good Friday, a day of execution yet not martyrdom, Jesus exhibits the ultimate sacrifice, servanthood taken to its outer limits. "Greater love hath no man than this, that a man lay down his life for his friends."[106] And it was not only his chosen band for whom he went to the Cross, but all of us as well, children yet unborn.

The Easter Vigil held in the darkness of Holy Saturday evening is perhaps the sacramental pinnacle of the Sacred Triduum. Yet somehow, its major sacrament is the first, not the last in the rites of Christian initiation. Baptism, the doorway to all sacramental life, including Eucharist, happens par excellence this night. It is enhanced with many other signs and symbols, rites, and readings, but the grafting of souls into the mystical Body of Christ is the main event. Is it a long service? Indeed, usually a minimum of two-hours long or longer. But when we reflect on how much time we spend

---

[105] A hymn by St. Thomas Aquinas speaks eloquently to this mystery: *Adoro te devote, latens Deitas. Quae sub his figuris, vere latitas.* (See *Hymnal 1982*, #314: "Humbly I adore thee, verity unseen, who thy glory hidest 'neath these shadows mean.")

[106] John 15:13 (KJV).

in front of one screen or another, we might well examine our conscience as to why we couldn't devote even three hours to such a sacred and signal event.

Palm Sunday presents an overview of the events to follow in the life of Christ. But, given such a glorious, even promising introduction, the following chapters seem totally inconsistent with such a bright beginning. Palm Sunday sounds a lot like the hoopla you hear at national political conventions, people wildly waving home-made signs (palm branches), and shouting out campaign slogans (hosannas).[107] It's already a done deal, a victory event! Our candidate has won the primary and will surely ace the general election, too. He'll *Ride on, Ride on in Majesty* to take his place as the long-awaited Messiah come to solve their every problem, right? After all, he is the King of the Jews, isn't he? Even Pilate supports that. "He'll make Jerusalem great again," they were thinking, now that they finally had their own politician!

But what in the world were they expecting from their Messiah? People expected a political leader, but political leadership style can vary widely. What were they thinking? Maybe something along these lines:

> We're all in for our man. He can do no wrong. He's a man of the people. We know him. We've seen him in action, campaigning in every town, holding "town hall meetings," right? He did so much good; he was so kind, and such a success! Everybody loves *Yeshua*, right? And so now it's time to "Crown Him with Many Crowns." He's the one to rid us of those rotten Romans, right, those foreigner rulers. Finally, we'll be able do our own thing.

---

107 Matthew 21:1-11.

Well, what's wrong with this picture? How does our *Table of Contents* go so horribly wrong? The *Introduction* sounded *great*—so positive, encouraging, and hopeful. Well, once again the *oligarchy*, those establishment fat cats weigh in. Mark's gospel says that

> The leading priests and the teachers of religious law were still looking for an opportunity to capture Jesus secretly and kill him.[108]

So, it must be that not quite everyone was on board this celebratory train.

And now *Yeshua's* people, his erstwhile silent majority (forget about their former spirited hymns and hosannas), have once more fallen mysteriously silent, very silent. Remember when Jesus was dining at Bethany and some gate-crashing female entered and spontaneously anointed him? Well, some formerly supportive people suddenly changed their tune:

> Some of those at the table were indignant. "Why waste such expensive perfume?" they asked. "It could have been sold for a year's wages and the money given to the poor!" So, they scolded [the woman] harshly.[109]

Harsh scolding and stinging criticism were now heard from the very same lips that were only recently singing "All Glory Laud and Honor." The tide turns.

Now even one of the twelve apostles, Judas Iscariot, finds himself no longer able to chant that hymn. He has chosen to sing a quite different tune:

---

108 Mark 14:1.
109 Mark 14:4-5.

> Then Judas Iscariot, one of the twelve disciples, went to the leading priests to arrange to betray Jesus to them. They were delighted when they heard why he had come, and they promised to give him money. So, he began looking for an opportunity to betray Jesus.[110]

What's happening? Where have all the strength and beauty in our Introduction to that book entitled *Holy Week* gone? *Hail, Thee, Festival Day!* It was all so positive, harmonious, so unmistakably in a major key. But harmony gives way to dissonance, eventually to outright cacophony. Major has modulated to minor. What might be next?

Jesus is about to celebrate Passover with his disciples. At table he reminds them that all is not well—that one of their very own brothers will betray him—somebody sitting right there with them tonight:

> In the evening Jesus arrived with the Twelve. As they were at the table eating, Jesus said, "I tell you the truth, one of you eating with me here will betray me." Greatly distressed, each one asked in turn, "Am I the one?" He replied, "It is one of you twelve who is eating from this bowl with me."[111]

The joyous music now becomes much more solemn as Jesus, presiding over His Last Supper, will institute the Holy Sacrifice of the Mass. His words "This is my Body, this is my Blood," would continue to echo down the centuries from the lips of his priests and bishops.

---

110   Mark 14:10-11.
111   Mark 14:17-20.

Amidst the gloom of betrayal which enabled an enraged establishment, Jesus decides to leave us Himself in the form of a meal—a gift until the end of time. A pivotal moment amidst impending doom with even more disappointment ahead. Although he said he never would, Peter denies Jesus three times trying to save his own skin. As Jesus contemplates his agony in the garden of Gethsemane, there is only more disappointment:

> They went to the olive grove called Gethsemane, and Jesus said, "Sit here while I go and pray." He took Peter, James, and John with him, and he became deeply troubled and distressed. He told them, "My soul is crushed with grief to the point of death. Stay here and keep watch with me."[112]

Peter, James, and John, three of Jesus' closest disciples, the ones he took with him to witness the Transfiguration, even now after so much time with the Lord, still don't get it. They can't identify with the agony Jesus is experiencing. They fail him in his hour of need, dozing off rather than *watching one hour*. Even they let Jesus down at this most *crucial* moment.

How can we reconcile such mixed messages? Wildly enthusiastic support, a triumphal procession, and then sudden abandonment of all support as things progressed. How could Jesus endure such fickle behavior?

But the more important question might be, how can you and I follow Jesus one moment and walk away from Him the next? Is there any effective antidote to fickle behavior? I believe there is, and it is a quite solid remedy indeed. Where can we find it? In the second chapter of Philippians,

---

[112] Mark 14:32-34.

there's a passage known as the "kenotic hymn."¹¹³ *Kenosis* in Greek means "emptying." *Kenosis* is the spiritual process by which the human being called Jesus was able to cope with the unanticipated vicissitudes of daily life, no matter how extreme. He was able to survive the cruelest reversals of fate by embracing the discipline of *kenosis*. Can we find hope in this for ourselves?

> Let the same mind be in you that was in Christ Jesus, who, though he was in the form of God, did not regard equality with God as something to be exploited, but emptied himself, taking the form of a slave, being born in human likeness. And being found in human form, he humbled himself and became obedient to the point of death—even death on a cross.¹¹⁴

---

113   Philippians 2:5-11.
114   Philippians 2:5-8.

ETERNITY

The undergraduate college I attended had a very beautiful, elegant library building. The only problem, partly due to its traditional architecture, was that you had to hike up an endless number steps to get inside. I'd never been much of an athlete, so to do library research I would just have to trudge up those never-ending steps. But as I trudged up the hill, I kept focusing on the inscription over the front entrance, reading over and over again the Latin words inscribed there:

> Ut cognoscant te solum verum Deum
> et quem misisti Iesum Christum.
>
> That they may know you, the only true God,
> and Jesus Christ, whom you have sent.[115]

This quotation is from the seventeenth chapter of John's gospel, known as the "Great High Priestly Prayer" of Jesus. According to that gospel, it is one of the last things Christ said before his arrest, conviction, passion, and death. This utterance, addressed to his heavenly Father, was in fact his last will and testament to humankind. But it always helps to look at any quotation in context. The inscribed words made up only the second half of a verse which begins:

> Haec est autem vita aeterna:
> And this is eternal life:

---

[115] John 17:3.

The beginning words of this verse identify the following words as Christ's definition of eternal life. "Eternal life is as follows" would be another way to put it. The second half of the verse tells exactly what Jesus means by eternal life. In his "Great High Priestly Prayer," Jesus had hoped for two things. First, he hoped to be able to bestow *eternal life* on all those whom the Father had given him.[116] Secondly, in the final words of this prayer, he expressed his hope that "[all humankind] may be one, as we are one."[117]

When you and I hear the words *eternal life*, we normally think of the *afterlife*, something that happens only after you die. But what did Jesus mean by the expression *eternal life*? When does it begin? When *could* it begin? More importantly, when does God *intend* eternal life to begin? At what point along life's continuum whether long or short? If our *physical life* clearly spans from birth to death, then does our *eternal life* just pick up where our physical life leaves off? That's what most people think. But I am suggesting an alternative view. Our theology teaches that the soul is immortal. Once conceived, the soul lives forever. Science teaches that when the physical body dies, our mortal life ceases. As long as we are alive our immortal soul and mortal body coexist. At physical death, our immortal soul continues to live on and exist in another dimensionality.

And so, to return to my original questions: when in the mind of Christ is eternal life supposed to begin? And precisely what did Jesus mean by *eternal life*? Jesus' first desire was to bestow it on all humankind. His definition of *eternal life* were written in the words I kept reading over and over again as I approached the library entrance: "That they may know you, the only true God, and Jesus Christ, whom you have sent."

---

116 John 17:2.
117 John 17:11.

That's how Christ defined *eternal life*. But do we have to wait until we're dead to achieve this state? To know God and Jesus Christ whom God had sent? Isn't that a bit late? Why wait till then? How will we ever be able to recognize Jesus in the afterlife if we've never known him here in this life? I'm pretty sure Jesus wanted us to get to know him quite well in this world before we are called to meet him in the next. And we do not mean *knowing about him* theologically but *knowing him* personally, having become well acquainted with the real presence of Jesus. Jesus wants us as his friends, not his experts.

Life is a continuum. Its continuity is guaranteed by the immortality of the soul. A few words from the preface of the Funeral Mass say it all:

> *Tuis enim fidelibus, Domine, vita mutatur non tollitur.*
>
> To your faithful servants, O Lord, life is changed, not ended.

The operative words are *changed, not ended*. After our mortal, physical life is done, the immortal life of the soul continues without interruption. Let us not waste another minute. Let's not procrastinate any longer. Eternal life is supposed to begin right now, not at some uncertain future date, and certainly not after we've taken our last breath. Enjoying a relationship with *the only true God and his Son, Jesus Christ* is what it's all about. Eternal life, kingdom life, is far too good to put off. If I haven't done so already, today's not any too soon.

EXPLETIVES

In some press articles you may see the bracketed words *[expletive deleted]*. Certain government documents have used this expression to disguise profanity in the original text. The phrase "expletive deleted" is especially reminiscent of the Watergate era,[118] when, in April 1974, President Nixon was ordered to turn over all his official tape recordings to the House Judiciary Committee. After Nixon had examined drafts of the transcriptions, he was shocked to discover how much profanity he had used. So, to cover these, he ordered every instance to be replaced with the bracketed phrase *[expletive deleted]*.

I'm not sure that every deleted remark would actually have qualified as *profanity* in the theological sense.[119] Profanity includes obscenity as well as irreligious, irreverent or blasphemous speech. What he ordered deleted was more likely *vulgarity,* or *cuss* words. Had the transcriptions gone forth in their raw, unedited state they might not exactly have qualified as "all the news that's fit to print."

In far less rarified circles than either the White House or the *New York Times*, church folk have for years had their own brand of expletives, theologically *profane* rather than *vulgar*. The commandment from Exodus, restated

---

118 The Watergate scandal was a political event occurring in the United States which involved the administration of President Richard Nixon from 1972 to 1974. It ultimately led to Nixon's resignation.

119 Exodus 20:7. "Thou shalt not take the name of the Lord in vain."

in Deuteronomy,[120] forbids the use of any non-religious reference to the divinity, for example yelling *God* as an expletive. The current cyber shorthand OMG could mean either "Oh, my goodness" or "Oh, my God!" Expressions such as *gee, gosh* or *golly* all derive from *God* but don't cross the line. If you hit your thumb instead of the nail while hammering and yell "God dammit, Jesus Christ" or any combination thereof, you are treading on thin ice. To invoke divinity carelessly or casually is to risk at least a *venial sin*.

When suddenly shocked or taken by surprise, a frequent Roman Catholic expletive used to be *Jesus, Mary, and Joseph*. That's right, the entire Holy Family was called upon. And these were definitely expletives, but not in the bad sense. They were spontaneous cries for help in distress.

And so, at this point you might be wondering, why we are talking about expletives? And furthermore, what might all of this have to do with the season of Advent? It's a segue to examine not only reference to Jesus but to have a look at his entire family. Whether one uses A.D. or C.E,[121] the entire world begins counting in our time from the birth of Jesus. And that birth involved not only Jesus, but Mary and Joseph as well. How did the phrase *Jesus, Mary, and Joseph!* ever became such a common, non-sinful expletive? Why did people ever need a triple, quasi-religious expletive? Here's how Matthew approaches that concept:

> Now the birth of Jesus the Messiah took place in this way. When his mother Mary had been engaged to Joseph, but before they lived together, she was found to be with child from the Holy Spirit.[122]

---

120 Deuteronomy 5:11.
121 A.D. stands for *anno Domini*, in the year of the Lord; C.E. stands for common era.
122 Matthew 1:18.

An engaged couple has, presumably, conceived a child out of wedlock. For us today, this would be no big deal. Marriages today often take place well after children are born into a family. But at the time of Jesus, no such liberal conventions were acceptable. Severe punishment awaited anyone, particularly women, who did anything out of the conventional order, who dared challenge the sacred sanctions of a legalistic society. With zero tolerance for any departure from tradition, good luck convincing anyone back then that Jesus had been *conceived by the Holy Spirit*,[123] as we now so readily pronounce in the liturgy. And therefore...

> Her husband Joseph, being a righteous man and unwilling to expose her to public disgrace, planned to dismiss her quietly.[124]

This verse says so much about the character of Joseph. Being *righteous*, like any other Jew, he would scrupulously try to observe the letter of the law. In those days, there was no wiggle room for interpretation of the law. For the Jewish people of the day, the Law was considered literal in meaning and primary in practice.

Mary and Joseph would not have been able to legally marry had she been pregnant. But Joseph was not inclined to judge or punish the woman he loved. He would not let her suffer the indignity of being shunned, or worse, stoned or otherwise punished for being with child. He was not inclined to *dismiss her quietly*, that is, unceremoniously and without fanfare. On the contrary, Joseph was kind and loving. Somehow, he was skeptical about the prevailing Pharisaical law-and-order mentality. This was not how Joseph interpreted life. He could not see letting his beloved

---

123 An article of faith in both the Apostles' Creed as well as the Nicene Creed.
124 Matthew 1:19.

Mary suffer needlessly. Giving birth would be pain enough. Nor would he waste his breath trying to convince some stiff-necked Pharisee about a miracle, only to have that stubborn legalist laugh in his face.

> But just when [Joseph] had resolved to do this [to dismiss her quietly], an angel of the Lord appeared to him in a dream and said, "Joseph, son of David, do not be afraid to take Mary as your wife, for the child conceived in her is from the Holy Spirit. She will bear a son, and you are to name him Jesus, for he will save his people from their sins."[125]

Joseph, like his bride Mary,[126] being open to the Lord, was able to hear an angel's message and take it seriously. That dream was loaded with content, including his son's name and mission: Jesus, Messiah, Savior, and Redeemer of humankind. If we accept the doctrine of the Virgin Birth[127] when we say "born of the Virgin Mary," then we see that this dream called Joseph to become the foster father of Jesus. The character of Joseph is clear from the get-go. He yields to the Holy Spirit. He listens to angels and takes them seriously. And he obeys. Rather than disown Mary, he carries out his assigned role bravely. He would have likewise been punished severely, had this out-of-wedlock pregnant couple become public. But Joseph was obedient to the Holy Spirit. His ears, his eyes, and his heart were all quite disposed to divine guidance. He chose to listen to God rather than lean on his own understanding.[128] Matthew's account continues:

---

125 Matthew 1: 20-21.
126 See Luke 1:46-55, the famous *Magnificat* of Mary's acceptance.
127 See both the Apostles' Creed and the Nicene Creed.
128 See Proverbs 3:5.

> All this took place to fulfill what had been spoken by the Lord through the prophet:
>
> "Look, the virgin shall conceive and bear a son, and they shall name him Emmanuel," which means, "God is with us." When Joseph awoke from sleep, he did as the angel of the Lord commanded him; he took her as his wife, but had no marital relations with her until she had borne a son; and he named him Jesus.[129]

Jesus, Mary and, Joseph! Now, a Holy Family. The child about to be born *for us and for our salvation*.[130] A virgin, a young woman who self-identified as the *handmaid of the Lord* chosen to be the mother of God's only son, an obscure teenager from a tawdry town who simply said *yes*. And then, who was this least-highlighted family member, Joseph? Quiet, reflective, holy, dedicated to justice and peace, this man was an early servant-leader. Oft forgotten, but like other unsung father-figures, one especially deserving of our accolade. Had Joseph answered the angel any differently, if he had responded like Zechariah,[131] ignoring or discounting the encounter, who knows what might have happened? Would there ever have been a *Holy Family* at all?

It is therefore not all that hard to understand why believers of bygone times used a more complete "holy" expletive when surprised or scared. They didn't blurt out God or Christ, but would hopefully exclaim *Jesus, Mary, and Joseph!*

---

[129] Matthew 1: 22-25.
[130] Nicene Creed.
[131] Luke 1: 68-79.

FICKLENESS

Southern California doesn't get much rain. Occasionally, there is a healthy dose of it. You can tell how rare it is in this region of the country, because the locals drive a little funny when it rains. They're just not used to it. They scramble around nervously in search of an umbrella. I have to say, I rejoice whenever there's a downpour. Now that's not to say I'd like to live in England or in the Pacific Northwest, but moderate rainfall can be a blessing in so many ways. I used to try to entertain people by suggesting that any sudden, unexpected deluge was really a spontaneous *Asperges*, Holy Water from above. But I'm afraid my ham-fisted attempt at an explanation fell on deaf ears, or that it simply didn't hold water.

Before the liturgical changes following the Second Vatican Council,[132] a *Rorate Caeli* Mass used to be celebrated very early on the Saturday mornings of Advent, occasionally even on weekdays as well. Before the Council, all masses were identified by the first words of their *introit* or entrance rite. The introit for the *Rorate Caeli* mass was taken from Isaiah. Anticipating Christmas, these opening words asked that the heavens open up and the clouds rain down *the just one*, namely the Messiah who had been promised to bring about justice and righteousness:

---

132   1962-1965.

> Rorate, caeli, desuper, et nubes pluant
> justum; aperiatur terra, et germinet
> Salvatorem, et justitia oriatur simul: ego
> Dominus creavi eum.
>
> Drop down dew, ye heavens, from above,
> and let the clouds rain the just: let the
> earth be opened, and bud forth a savior:
> and let justice spring up together:
> I the Lord have created him.[133]

In years where the heavens do open up, a sustained drought finally gets at least some temporary relief. Prayers are answered and even a short-term soaking does some good. Can we understand now why every Advent we ask that the skies open up? Don't we desperately need the waters of heaven to open up at least annually and irrigate our arid souls? Even a short downpour would be better than endless drought.

Five chapters earlier in Isaiah we see another agricultural text about rain, crops, and growth. This scripture refers to us as *grass*:

> A voice says, "Cry out!"
> And I said, "What shall I cry?"
> All people are grass, their constancy is
> like the flower of the field.
>
> The grass withers, the flower fades,
> when the breath of the Lord blows upon it;
> surely the people are grass.
>
> The grass withers, the flower fades;
> but the word of our God will stand forever.[134]

---

[133] Isaiah 45:8 (DRA).
[134] Isaiah 40:6-8.

The reference to *constancy* reminds us of the *inconstancy* or *fickleness* which is part-and-parcel of our human nature. One Eucharistic Prayer admits as much:

> Sanctify us also that we may faithfully receive this holy Sacrament, and serve you in unity, constancy, and peace.[135]

Constancy, consistency, regularity, reliability: all challenging concepts these. Grass by its very nature is *fickle*. Give it enough water and sunlight, feed it, and weed it, and you might eventually have your own golf course. Neglect regular watering, skip fertilizing or weeding, just leave it be, and see what happens. You'll have the polar opposite of a championship golf course. Before long, the result will be brown, parched, patchy, and eventually dead grass. Neglect leads to slow death. Today's fertile landscape can become tomorrow's unsightly desert. Any possible connection here with the spiritual life?

Preventing brown-out and desiccation is what the Advent cry of *Rorate caeli* is all about. We're begging God to rain down upon us *the* ultimate Holy Water, those living, saving waters of Jesus Christ. And we're not asking for a light sprinkling, an *Asperges*, a mere drizzle, a little dab. Unfortunately, not. Because in this case, just *a little dab won't do you*. We're asking for an all-out cloud burst, the downright drenching our spiritual landscape so desperately lacks.

During these days before Christmas, we confess our aridity, our dryness, our parchedness of soul, and yes, our inconstancy. Once again, as we await the Messiah, we admit our fickleness and outright vacillation in our relationship with God. We ask for relief. So far, at least, our lack of consistency has not risen to the level of our total undoing.

---

135 *BCP 1979*, p. 363.

Fortunately, we're still hanging on and our God is a patient God.

> The Lord is not slow about his promise, as some think of slowness, but is patient with you, not wanting any to perish, but all to come to repentance.[136]

Why does God wait for us to come around? Because God loves us. And God's time is not our time:

> With the Lord one day is like a thousand years, and a thousand years are like one day.[137]

God is prepared to wait a thousand years, even two or three thousand, for us to come to repentance, to turn over that new leaf. Every year we await the birth of Christ for less than four short weeks. But although brief, this holy season is a spiritual exercise in waiting, *purposefully* waiting for the cloudburst of the Messiah.

A popular hit song and movie from the 1950s bore the title "Singin' in the Rain." The origin of both music and lyrics were anything but happy. They were born in an environment of a sad and hopeless lament. Words and music were composed by Johnny Bragg, a seventeen-year-old African-American kid, unjustly jailed in the Tennessee State Penitentiary. It was Johnny's lament as he sadly yet dutifully went about his assigned tasks while incarcerated for a crime he never committed. If you and I were to sing the words and music of the *Rorate caeli* today, how would we say we're feeling? Would it be sad or glad, or maybe even mad? When we ask God for our own personal heavenly cloudburst, how are we *singin' in*

---

136 2 Peter 3:9.
137 2 Peter 3:8.

the rain? Is it a peaceful chant or a hopeless lament? Could we hope for it to be a joyful response to being drenched with Holy Water? We are asked that same rhetorical question a few verses later in the same epistle:

> What sort of persons are we supposed to become? How are we to lead holy and godly lives?[138]

Will I choose to sing *joyfully* in the Advent rain? Am I willing to submit to a true *baptism of repentance*? Am I at least willing to try to turn around and face the Christ Child at his birth? Advent affords us an auspicious, grace-filled moment to seek *metanoia*, to turn around and walk toward Bethlehem.

---

138 2 Peter 3:11.

FORGIVENESS

Most Sundays bear rather prosaic, uninspiring titles on the liturgical calendar like "the Fourth Sunday after Pentecost" or "the Second Sunday in Lent." One Sunday, however, hasn't only one title but several, namely the Fourth Sunday in Lent. Lent, a longish liturgical season, is designed to afford more time for reflection and repentance, a time to look deeply into our spiritual lives and make appropriate course corrections. From time to time, we need to turn around, have a change of heart, experience *metanoia*. The fourth Sunday, marking the half-way point, is timely for some mid-course correction. It's also an auspicious moment to set aside the more intense spiritual navel-gazing Lent is all about. While the usual liturgical color for Lent is violet, on the fourth Sunday there is a rubrical option to use the color rose. Why rose? Because it is considered a muted, softer, gentler, more joyful variation on the color violet.

What other names are there for this curious Sunday? *Rose Sunday* is perhaps most obvious, but *Rose Sunday* is not exclusive to Lent.[139] Another title, familiar in the United Kingdom, is *Mothering Sunday*, sometimes also called *Mother's Day* there. It occurs exactly three weeks before Easter Sunday, usually late March or early April. Mothering Sunday was originally a time when people would return to the church of their infant baptism or where they had

---

[139] The mid-Sunday in Advent, namely the third Sunday, also enjoys the rose option and may therefore claim the title of Rose Sunday as well.

attended services as children. This therefore meant that families would be reunited when they returned to where they grew up. In time, young people working as servants in large houses would get a holiday on Mothering Sunday to visit their mother. Occasionally, they would bring a gift of food or some article of used clothing discarded by their employers. Naturally, in time these customs all evolved but somehow Mothering Sunday always retained the basics of visiting one's mother and bringing a gift. In times past, during Lent Christians worldwide would forgo sweets, rich foods, and especially meat. On Mothering Sunday in the British Isles, however, the fast was relaxed so families could at least enjoy the traditional Simnel cake[140] baked for the occasion.

A natural by-product of such family reunions must have been the opportunity for estranged family members to reconcile. Most families, especially extended ones, can become quite large and diverse as children grow into adulthood. Setting aside at least one Sunday a year for all to come from far and wide could certainly go a long way toward mending broken relationships. That was easier for people in the British Isles years ago than it is for us today. Back in the day, family tended to settle pretty close to home and so early life in Great Britain presented fewer barriers to celebrating Mothering Sunday. The USA is larger and more spread out from coast to coast than England, Scotland and Wales combined. But it is also true that travel booked in advance is reasonable and readily available. Families *could* gather quite easily, if they wanted to. For most North Americans, Thanksgiving and/or Christmas do what Mothering Sunday used to in Great Britain.

---

140 A Simnel cake is a light fruit cake covered with marzipan and with a layer of marzipan baked into the middle of the cake. Traditionally, Simnel cakes are decorated with 11 or 12 balls of marzipan, representing the 11 disciples and, sometimes, Jesus Christ. One legend says that the cake was named after Lambert Simnel who worked in the kitchens of Henry VII of England sometime around the year 1500.

Does the New Testament speak at all about an occasion for estranged family members to reconcile? Indeed, I believe it does. To be inclusive, any talk of a *Mothering Sunday* should lead us also to ask about a *Fathering Sunday*. I know of neither a historical nor a liturgical precedent for such, but it would only be fair to entertain the concept. I'm suggesting that we celebrate *Fathering Sunday* when the parable of the *Prodigal Son*[141] is read.

Sometimes words like *prodigal* get so closely associated with a scripture that people come to believe that the word itself is actually there. The same is true for the phrase *Good Samaritan*. The word *good* is not used either to describe this generous fellow. He is characterized as *merciful*, as more accurately expressed by the German reference to him.[142] Our basic linguistic problem is that the younger son is not the *prodigal* one; his father is.

But what does *prodigal* actually mean? The dictionary defines the noun *prodigy* primarily as "a person, especially a child or youth who has extraordinary talent or ability, as in *a musical prodigy*. The adjective *prodigious* is defined as "extraordinary in size, amount, extent, degree, force, etc., as in a *prodigious* research grant." A related meaning is "wonderful or marvelous," as in a *prodigious feat* or in the more accurate sense of this parable, his *prodigious father* put on a *prodigious feast*. The noun *prodigy* and its first derivative adjective *prodigious* speak of *abundance* not *paucity*.

When the second derivative adjective *prodigal* is heard by speakers of American English, they immediately think of the familiar common title of this parable, The *Prodigal* Son. But following the original line of meaning of the words *prodigy*

---

141 Luke 15.
142 German bibles refer to him as *der barmherzige Samariter* (the merciful Samaritan).

and *prodigious*, the more accurate first meaning of *prodigal* would be "giving or yielding profusely or lavishly," and therefore in the context of this parable, *the prodigal father*. Only as a last listing is the commonly accepted definition of *prodigal*: wastefully or recklessly extravagant, as in *the prodigal son*. But who in this parable was the more recklessly extravagant?

The father in this parable deserves a *Fathering Sunday* because he was truly *prodigal*, not his wayward younger son. The father was the *prodigious* one, literally *prodigal* in the extravagant reception and treatment of the son whom he had once deemed dead and now who had returned to life. This is family reconciliation at its best, with no score kept for any past offenses, whether peccadilloes or felonies. No lecture. No silent treatment. Just a warm, *prodigious* welcome home accompanied by an over-the-top banquet. The father's response is so *prodigious* that the elder son is at first blown away by it. He can't explain the music, the dancing, the feast, the finest wines being served. He never expected his father to be quite so *prodigious* for anyone, least of all his wastrel brother. But isn't that a vintage display of how God operates?

> What do you think? If a shepherd has a hundred sheep, and one of them has gone astray, does he not leave the ninety-nine on the mountains and go in search of the one that went astray? And if he finds it, truly I tell you, he rejoices over it more than over the ninety-nine that never went astray.[143]

---

143 Matthew 18:12-13.

The elder son, the father reminded him, had always stayed home with him. He was sensible and graced enough not to pursue the path his younger brother did. He was one of the "ninety-nine" who were in no need of a physician.[144] His ne'er-do-well brother was less fortunate. Yielding to temptation, he strayed.

A well-known yet worn-out poem beginning "Roses are red: violets are blue" has endured such romantic endings as "I dream of ways to be with you," or "You make the world better by just being you." We might question the first part, that "roses are red," because all roses are certainly not red. On *Rose Sundays* they are pink. In the context of the forgiveness taught in this parable, I would like to name these *Roses of Reconciliation*. Having looked a bit more closely at the lexicon, we can now see that from three words *prodigal, prodigious,* and *prodigy* two distinct meanings emerge from this parable. For reconciliation, forgiveness, and restored relationships to take place, a great deal of grace is required because, "there, but for the grace of God, go I." In God's Greenhouse, the Rose of Reconciliation blooms ever pink and ever lovely.

---

144 Mark 2:17. "When Jesus heard this, he said to them, 'Those who are well have no need of a physician, but those who are sick; I have come to call not the righteous but sinners."

FREEDOM

If you and I were playing a game of word association, I might say the word *free*. What word would you say next? Free—what? And if we were playing with other people, undoubtedly several different responses would be forthcoming.

Whenever I hear *free*, my ears perk up. I think of such delightful synonyms as *gratis*, no charge, complimentary, or even *freebie*. But popular wisdom claims there is no *free lunch*, in other words, *freebies* are fictional. Regardless how enticing the sales pitch, the invite to a steak dinner at a fancy restaurant, which for dessert will serve you a *free* investment seminar, will cost you your entire evening. Every advertisement, it would seem, sports its own peculiar price tag. That *free* steak dinner will not only cost you the time to listen to their canned *spiel* but also they won't let you out the door without more high pressure tactics. A *free lunch* or any other freebie has its own pricetag. There are always strings fluttering in the breeze. When an item is advertised "*on sale up to 50% off*," my standard response is, "50% off what?" Usually, it's off some inflated, marked-up MSRP! While that might sound like a cynic talking, so be it.

Nonetheless I confess, I'm always drawn to what at least *looks* like a good deal. And I must confess, I do love to haggle over price, especially with car dealers, as I hope against hope to strike some windfall bargain. Nowadays, that's way harder than it used to be. Well, what then *is* actually free? What truly bears no price tag at all? Is there some commodity I never need haggle over? Is there actually something I never *can* haggle over? Short answer: yes.

A remarkable example of liturgical poetry is the canticle[145] known as the *Song of Zechariah.*[146] Its message is so significant that it was selected to be the preferred canticle at Morning Prayer. Why was this particular canticle selected? And how does it relate to the theme of freedom?

There is some important history that took place before the *Canticle of Zechariah* was first sung. Earlier in the first chapter of Luke[147] the priest Zechariah—while performing his assigned temple duties—was informed by the angel Gabriel that he and his aged wife Elizabeth were about to become parents. Zechariah reacted cynically. He gave Gabriel quite a bit of attitude. He was totally unprepared to receive such an outlandish message. But the temple priest Zechariah forgot one small detail: it wasn't Gabriel's message but God's. So, bottom line, he was unwilling to trust God. And for his haughty response, Zechariah was silenced until the birth of his son. After his son had been born and was brought to temple for dedication, Zechariah confirmed that his name was to be John. From this point on, Zechariah began once again to cooperate with God's grace, and so his speech was restored. He was now speaking God's word, rather than his own. A miracle now began to unfold. Zechariah, his tongue now loosened, chanted the pristine, prophetic words of the canticle which would henceforth forever bear his name.

In this single, inspired a-ha moment, Zechariah was enabled to envision two crucial events in salvation history: (1) the long-awaited arrival of the Messiah promised for

---

145 A canticle is literally a short song. Other significant liturgical canticles are the "Song of Mary" (Luke 1:46-55) and the "Song of Simeon" (Luke 2:29-32).
146 Luke 1:68-79.
147 Luke 1:13-20.

centuries in Hebrew scripture; and (2) the crucial supporting role his infant son was to play in the ongoing drama of salvation history. His infant son, John the Baptist, would be the one to identify his cousin *Yeshua ha-Mashiach*, Jesus the Messiah. Inspired by poetic, prophetic utterance, Zechariah restates three times what the chosen people were waiting for, *freedom*, and who was about to deliver it:

> Blessed be the Lord, the God of Israel;
> he has come to his people and set them free.[148]

> Through his holy prophets he promised of old, that he would save us from our enemies, from the hands of all who hate us.[149]

> This was the oath he swore to our father Abraham, to set us free from the hands of our enemies, free to worship him without fear, holy and righteous in his sight. all the days of our life.[150]

But one might inquire, liberation from what? Freedom from whom? How were the chosen people being held back? Who were their natural or supernatural enemies? On a more personal plane, who or what are *our* enemies? Who or what is holding us back from accepting, embracing, and moving forward with the mission and ministry God has given us? Zechariah prophesies that his son's ministry was to be that of Jesus' precursor. Addressing his infant son tenderly yet directly, Zechariah—now speaking for God rather than himself—announces his mission and ministry:

---

148 Luke 1:68.
149 Luke 1:70-71.
150 Luke 1:73-75.

> You, my child, shall be called the prophet of the Most High, for you will go before the Lord to prepare his way, To give people knowledge of salvation by the forgiveness of their sins.[151]

He foretells that his son John would fearlessly proclaim a *baptism of repentance*, the call to radical reorientation of life and change of heart. John, later baptizing in the Jordan, would dispose people to recognize Jesus as the one born *for us and for our salvation*.[152] Finally, someone would be coming to deliver on the centuries-old promises of prophets. Zechariah, at the highpoint of his poetic prowess, imagines what the ministry of *Yeshua ha-Mashiach* might look like:

> In the tender compassion of our God the dawn from on high shall break upon us, to shine on those who dwell in darkness and the shadow of death, and to guide our feet into the way of peace.[153]

The beautiful Canticle of Zechariah suggests some questions worth pondering. What are *we* afraid of? Whom do *we* fear? What makes *us* apprehensive? As God's chosen people today who are awaiting the Messiah, what are *we* afraid of? What are we seeking to escape from? The first verse of the hymn "Come, thou long-expected Jesus"[154] prays "from our fears and sins release us / let us find our rest in thee." Fears and sins. Who wouldn't love to experience *release* from both, and at no cost? Now that would be a deal worth looking at!

In his Inaugural Address of March 4th 1933, Franklin

---

151 Luke 1:76-77.
152 *BCP 1979*, p. 358, The Nicene Creed.
153 Luke 1:78-79.
154 *Hymnal 1982* #66.

Delano Roosevelt made a well-known, profound observation about the trials and tribulations confronting the nation. FDR said wisely that "we have nothing to fear but fear itself." To this wise insight I'd add another from the New Testament:

> Such love has no fear, because perfect love expels all fear. If we are afraid, it is for fear of punishment, and this shows that we have not fully experienced his perfect love.[155]

Or in other words:

> There is no fear in love [dread does not exist], but full-grown (complete, perfect) love turns fear out of doors and expels every trace of terror! For fear brings with it the thought of punishment, and [so] he or she who is afraid has not reached the full maturity of love [is not yet grown into love's complete perfection].[156]

Naturally, when Gabriel just dropped in unannounced, Zechariah got pretty scared. He was by nature rather disbelieving, mistrustful, maybe even cynical. He was overly skeptical about this so-called unannounced angel's message. But eventually, after enduring the penalty of nine months in silent reflection, he came around to learn that he could safely abandon fear and surrender to God's love. Finally, Zechariah had discovered *the perfect love which casts out fear*. You and I are most likely looking for that same kind of love. Perhaps it may become for us, each in our own way, *new every morning*.[157]

---

155 1 John 4:18 (NLT).
156 1 John 4:18 (AMP).
157 Hymn "New Every Morning Is The Love" by John Keble (1792-1866).

Fruitfulness

Have you ever played golf or even "played at it?" If so, you may be familiar with the good old Irish surname of *Mulligan*. You remember, don't you? The guy famous for taking that do-over shot that doesn't count on the score card.

Well, almost any season of the church year is a good one to work on our "spiritual" golf game. Well, how does one practice, warm-up before actually going out on the course itself? Most regulation golf courses have putting greens and chipping areas where one can practice shorter shots while waiting around for a tee time. It's always that extra putt or wild wedge shot that can run up your score card. Some courses also have their own driving ranges where you can break out those woods and practice long drives. Most even moderately strong golfers are able to propel the ball pretty far but it's usually those more finely-tuned short-distance shots that tend to run up your score. And golf is one game where you want to score as low as possible. Great golfers must be strong enough to whack the ball hard and straight down the fairway. Yet they must also be able to handle a pitching wedge or a putter as delicately as a surgeon would a scalpel. I don't know why, but the scripture about being wily as snakes and gentle as doves comes to mind here.[158]

Well, how closely does one's spiritual journey resemble a golf game? What are the putts, chips, and drives we practice

---

158   Matthew 10:16.

before the real game? How important are those practice shots? How do I go about honing my skills in the spiritual golf game of life? What sort of golf clinic might I visit to help me up my game? In regulation golf, 72 is par, a number adjustable to one's *handicap*. But unless you are a frequent, serious golfer (not a duffer like me) you probably don't even know your handicap. I played so irregularly that I never gave that issue a thought. If my score card ever added up to 72 after just nine holes, I would have been shouted several alleluias. When does my spiritual golf game ever get up to par? How can I honestly assess my progress? Based on frequent past performance, do I have any idea of my true handicap? How could I improve that number, whatever it might be? And perhaps, more to the point, what sort of performance does God expect from me on the course? Does he love duffers as much as pros? What does he think of Mulligans?

Some scriptures both *warn* us as well as *encourage* us. While taking these warnings to heart, I ought never abandon hope of improving. I need to be aware of what God expects, literally, where God is coming from as he walks beside me along the fairways of life. One epistle revisits the Old Testament scene where the Israelites were not only ungrateful but disobedient to *Yahweh*. They had finally pushed the envelope too far:

> [Finally] God was not pleased with most of them, and they were struck down in the wilderness. Now these things occurred as examples for us, so that we might not desire evil as they did.[159]

At some point, we must bear in mind that even God's patience gives out. In golf, a cardinal virtue is patience:

---

159 1 Corinthians 10:5-6.

patience with oneself, patience with the game itself, all the while keeping a cool head. But, because God is God, does that then mean that God's patience is without limit? Is there ever a breaking point? Both the Hebrew Bible as well as the New Testament are pretty clear on this. And yet there's an Isaiah passage that Matthew repeats word-for-word, a signature statement opening another window into how God deals with us and ultimately into the nature of God:

> A bruised reed he will not break, and a
> smoldering wick he will not snuff out.[160]

Most of us play the golf game of life with our own distinct handicaps. To one extent or another, we all qualify as bruised reeds or smoldering wicks. One day we might be somewhat spiritually alive but not burning very brightly. Our dimly burning wick is literally but a sneeze away from being extinguished. Sometimes don't I just feel so bruised and scarred that I could never even imagine becoming whole and healthy again? But divinity won't snuff out my humanity, no matter what my handicap. No, God desires to help me to wholeness, to the *more abundant life*[161] Jesus promised. A parable from Luke again demonstrates God's abiding patience and optimism:

> Then [Jesus] told this parable: "A man
> had a fig tree planted in his vineyard;
> and he came looking for fruit on it and
> found none. So, he said to the gardener,
> 'See here! For three years I have come
> looking for fruit on this fig tree, and still
> I find none. Cut it down! Why should it be
> wasting the soil?'"[162]

---

160 Isaiah 42:3; Matthew 12:20.
161 John 10:10.
162 Luke 13:6-7.

The landowner's initial impulse amounts to saying "get rid of this useless, stupid thing that'll never produce anything. It's just taking up precious real estate." But God the gardener has a different take on the matter:

> [The gardener] replied, "Sir, let it alone for one more year, until I dig around it and fertilize it. If it bears fruit next year, well and good; but if not, you can cut it down."[163]

Our Divine Gardener believes in His plantings. He is confident that what He has planted can potentially turn productive. Fortunately, unlike the stock market, God does not estimate future productivity based on past performance. God does not have some kind of divine scorecard on which to record my unproductive past and hold it against me. God looks upon his creation with a perpetually optimistic eye. God is always prepared for me to begin again, to start over, to try again. And I would confess that during my lifetime God has offered me more than one Mulligan.

Some of the Israelites indeed went too far and got punished for it. But God hopes we'll get it right, and never be so foolish as to presume on his mercy.[164] He gave the Israelites *forty years* to get it right, biblical code for an indefinite but seriously long time. But despite this generous extension, they still didn't. What's worse, they often refused to listen. There *are* consequences for trying God's patience too far. How can we forget Jesus' response to Satan about reckless behavior? "Do not put the Lord your God to the test."[165] No, indeed we dare not test God's patience by playing a hastily scheduled, carelessly executed, ill-prepared, and generally lackluster

---

163 Luke 13:8-9.
164 See Psalm 95:10-11.
165 Matthew 4:7; Luke 4:12.

spiritual golf game. God is calling me to engage in serious golf practice and is giving me way more than forty days to work on it. How can I forget the generosity of God, the ultimate gardener and golf pro, who is so patient with this novice, who wants me to slow down and luxuriate in his love? He will help me with those long shots as well as the shorter ones, shall we say, the more delicate maneuvers out of the sand traps of life? Like that barren fig tree, you and I might not have been all that spiritually productive recently. Perhaps we bore next to no spiritual fruit. Maybe we haven't scored all that well in the game of life, either. But God is somehow always around, standing by, walking the golf course beside me, coaching, nourishing, encouraging, and affirming me—until both my soil and my game improve.

GENEROSITY

That Gospel story[166] about the rich young man who ran up to Jesus all excited always bothered me when I was a teenager. It bothered me a lot.

I must confess something. I always wanted to become a priest, probably since I was about eight. That desire really began to grow in high school, a Jesuit prep, i.e., one belonging to the Society of Jesus. In those days, lay teachers were few and far between. Jesuit priests, brothers, and *scholastics* (seminarian interns) were absolutely plentiful. I commuted to school by train, arriving early enough to attend a daily 8:15 a.m. Mass there.

My uncle was a priest, but not a Jesuit. He was a diocesan or secular priest, one who didn't belong to any order like the Jesuits, Dominicans, Franciscans or Benedictines. He was simply a parish priest, and a good one.

The Oxford Movement brought back to the Church of England—and later to the Episcopal Church USA—religious orders such as Benedictines, Dominicans, and Franciscans. Diocesan bishops regularly give permission for new orders to be founded. Each has its own specific charism or special gift for ministry, for example prison ministry. While Episcopal monks and nuns do help out in parishes, their major focus is on carrying out their charism, not developing congregational life.

---

166 Mark 10: 17-31.

Maybe I was more intellectually suited to become a Jesuit rather than a diocesan parish priest. I loved teaching, research, and academic life in general. The Jesuits would probably have sent me on for doctoral studies, but as my life unfolded, I went on anyway to get a doctorate and become a university professor. Most Jesuits have advanced degrees beyond degrees in theology, many becoming physicians, lawyers, scientists or even politicians! Before the pope forbade it, there was actually a Jesuit serving as a U.S. Senator.

But another confession: I had one slight problem about signing up with the Jesuits. You see, I was the rich young man in that story.

Adopted as an only child into a wealthy family with parents already in their mid-forties, I was from infancy truly blessed. Family holidays with numerous aunts, uncles, and cousins were regularly held in our big beautiful English Tudor home.

So, can you perhaps see my slight problem a bit more clearly? Yes, that's right: I was the rich young man in that story.

As much as I might have been more suited to become a highly educated Jesuit, there was no way I was signing away my inheritance. I wasn't about to part with all the expensive furniture, including my Steinway grand, and all those oriental rugs, not even to mention the considerable real estate holdings my mother had acquired. Before even temporary vows, I would have had to dispose of any possessions in my name. I couldn't even imagine going *that* route.

You see, I was, in every sense of the word, the rich young man in that story, a guy *attached to*, or rather *possessed by*, material wealth. I was unwilling to trust God or the Jesuits to provide for my needs. Sadly, my *wants* always superseded my *needs*.

And so, eventually I became a *diocesan* priest, following in my uncle's footsteps. He owned a small house, drove a modest automobile, had a bank account, a few stock investments, even owned sports clothes and a set of golf clubs for his annual vacations.

My decision-making process could have been entitled *All This and Heaven, too.*[167] How could I have grown so materialistic, so self-centered, so greedy? How come I wouldn't trust God to provide for me even better than my parents had? Even worse, I'd heard this Gospel read in church year after year, but obviously it had gone in one ear and out the other.

My profile closely matched that of the rich young man. We each felt compelled to hang on to material wealth. Sharing with others, trusting God, had its limits. Each of us was eager to rattle off our good behavior to Jesus, while in the next breath politely inquiring how we might gain even more. What would it take to *inherit the Kingdom*? That was simply code for "how do I get my market share of your apparently successful enterprise?"

When Jesus explained what it would take, the rich man registered profound disappointment. His face fell. The entrance fee? Radical stewardship of self. Jesus was asking him whether he was willing to surrender *all* his earthly possessions, just like someone seeking to enter a religious order.

This encounter really all boils down to one simple word: *stewardship.* If you think about it for a while, you'll realize we don't *own* anything. What we think we *possess,* we only lease for a lifetime. A curmudgeon once commented that he'd never seen a hearse towing a U-Haul trailer! On appropriate stewardship of our material resources, Deuteronomy puts it this way:

---

167 "All This and Heaven, Too" was a 1940's American drama based on Rachel Field's 1938 novel by the same title.

> Then to the place the Lord your God will choose as a dwelling for his Name—there you are to bring everything I command you: …. your tithes and special gifts, and all the choice possessions you have vowed to the Lord.[168]

I don't have to sign it all over, disown what I don't own anyway, live the abstemious existence of a monk or a nun. That vocation is for the few. But whether I'm rich or poor or somewhere in-between, what is God calling me to give? The word *charity* originally meant *love, agape* love.[169] One Christmas carol says it all:[170]

> What can I give Him, poor as I am?
> If I were a shepherd, I would bring a lamb.
> If I were a wise man, I would do my part.
> Yet what can I give Him? Give Him my heart.

---

168 Deuteronomy 12:11.
169 ἀγαπάω is Greek for "I love, wish well, care about, am willing to sacrifice for."
170 "In the Bleak Midwinter."

HOUSECLEANING

Salvation history begins with Creation.[171] Yet somehow, God's grand plan goes awry. In a place of supreme beauty and divine order, bad advice leads to poor choices and ultimately to outright disobedience. To restore the balance between God and humankind now thrown-off-kilter by the first two people God ever created, restoration would call for a Redeemer, someone who could reestablish that proper balance. Such a one is referred to as the *Messiah*, or in Hebrew, *Yeshua ha-Mashiach*.

From the moment when Mary said "yes" to Gabriel, the eternal spirit of *Yahweh* began to take on human flesh within her. The Incarnation was only the beginning. When, by an action of the Holy Spirit, Jesus was conceived within Mary's womb, God could no longer remain aloof from humankind as pure spirit. In the person of Jesus, God would now be forever human as well as forever divine. In the person of Jesus, humanity and divinity were perpetually fused, forever united, eternally commingled. With the arrival of the Babe of Bethlehem, the pure spirit veil of the Trinity had been permanently pierced. God could no longer be accurately described as *pure spirit*. The long-awaited Messiah would be born as God-in-Christ, inhabiting a divine as well as a human nature, in every sense, *true God and true man*.

---

[171] Genesis 1:1.

Like Mary, you and I also have the opportunity to *ponder these events in our hearts,* but only over one shorter-than-usual month rather than the nine long months Mary had. We must rapidly assimilate this experience within the hectic, consumer-driven month of December. And amidst such frenetic hubbub, who can find adequate time for quiet reflection?

But like anything else worthwhile preparing for, we need our December to go quite differently. We are in desperate need of some time for intentional reflection. We need some space to be calm, quiet, and thoughtful. Without that, December can pass us by and become squandered spiritually, if we allow ourselves to be overtaken in the pursuit of *retail therapy.* Buying more stuff, even for others, is no therapy at all. It is an outright distraction from the religious reality of the Incarnation. The Babe of Bethlehem cannot be properly prepared for by wasting precious hours in shopping malls or by shopping on line. The Holy Infant is no fan of the frenetic. The Holy Family would prefer we invest at least some of these twenty-four days reflecting, anticipating, and preparing to welcome an infant about to alter the future course human history.

The administration building in a parish I once served desperately needed updating. Another victim of the deferred maintenance of church properties, it too had been sorely neglected. It needed a major make-over, to put it mildly. But as you probably know, more than 85% of the effort going into any renovation is expended in prep work. Without proper preparation of the surface, any paint job will result in a mess. I believe this principle of painstaking preparation holds true for any project involving renewal or restoration.

To facilitate matters in this run-down parish building, we rented a dumpster. We threw out stuff that had accumulated over decades. To a certain extent, you might say we were "casting away the works of darkness" by dumping the accumulated debris of years gone by. We were ridding ourselves of the scary *ghosts of Christmas past*, while preparing for the intervention of the Holy Ghost into the course of salvation history.

We scrubbed down walls and ceilings; we trashed worn-out carpeting. We took down every tacky announcement, every dated wall hanging. We needed a fresh start, a new perspective, a new outlook on parish community life. How would our future look after such a radical cleanup exercise? While it's always somewhat of a relief to abandon the past, it's likewise generally a bit daunting to anticipate the future. Is it possible for us to fashion a spiritual icon out of the experience of refreshing a building? Any kind of effective renovation, as we noted, entails hard work, much heavy lifting driven by a healthy dose of determination. What prep work would you and I need to anticipate, if we were to make twenty-four days really worthwhile? In four steps, the opening prayer for the first Sunday of Advent answers that:

1. Toss off your old, dark, shabby clothing.
2. Put on bright, sturdy new garments.
3. Get ready *now*, while we're still here on earth, to welcome Jesus.
4. Get ready to meet Jesus *later* on judgment day.

Advent disciplines our focus on both the *beginning* as well as on the *end*. We joyfully anticipate Jesus' *first arrival* at Christmas, as we simultaneously soberly prepare for his *second coming*.[172] Throughout Advent, the readings

---

172 Matthew 25:31-32. "When the Son of Man comes in his glory, and all the angels with him, then he will sit on the throne of his glory. All the nations will be gathered before him, and he will separate people one from another as a shepherd separates the sheep from the goats."

constantly remind us that we are preparing to encounter Christ in two distinct roles, often referred to as the Alpha and the Omega, the first and the last, the virtual bookends of salvation history. Christ, who first appears in swaddling clothes will later appear in judicial robes. As each new church year begins, we are given the overview. We are reminded that the Son of Man must play a comprehensive role in salvation history. The savior born "for us and for our salvation"[173] is likewise the one appointed to render a verdict on our lives.[174] That uniquely divine balance between justice and mercy is beautifully expressed in a familiar psalm:

> Mercy and truth have met each other;
> justice and peace have kissed.[175]

Well, just how then do we begin the process of tossing off our old, worn-out clothing in favor of fresh new garments? The opening prayer referred to earlier was borrowed and adapted from the Letter to the Romans:

> The night is almost gone; the day of
> salvation will soon be here. So, remove
> your dark deeds like dirty clothes,
> and put on the shining armor of right
> living.[176]

The first step involves ripping off and firing into the dumpster all the threadbare rags of our darkest deeds. The second step suggests how and with what we are to clothe ourselves instead: respectfully, with dignity, we are to put on the protective clothing of light.

---

[173] See the Nicene Creed, *BCP 1979*, p. 358.
[174] See the Nicene Creed, *BCP 1979*, p. 359: "He will come again in glory to judge the living and the dead, and his kingdom will have no end."
[175] Psalm 85:11.
[176] See Romans 12:12. The wording of the Vulgate is even more pictorial than that in English: "Abjiciamus ergo opera tenebrarum et induamur arma lucis."

All trash, especially toxic waste, is to be discarded forthwith. Not smart to keep this stuff around, especially if you're wearing it, if it has contact with your skin. Toxic waste is initially corrosive and ultimately deadly. The Latin word *abjiciamus* means to *reject* that which has now become *abject* in our lives. Only after we have doffed the burden of our dark deeds will we then be ready to don the buoyant holy vesture of our newfound *pearl of great price*.[177]

Di-vesting and re-investing suggests bold imagery. And this challenging task is precisely what we're called to undertake during Advent: discard darkness and embrace light. Isn't it time to prepare now for our next thorough pre-Christmas housecleaning, for that fresh start and new beginning?

---

[177] Matthew 13:45-46. "Again, the kingdom of heaven is like unto a merchant man, seeking goodly pearls: Who, when he had found one pearl of great price, went and sold all that he had, and bought it." (KJV).

Identity

Christmas always brings me great personal happiness. There has been somewhat of a running debate whether Christmas or Easter is the more preeminent feast. For me, that's a fairly easy question to answer. Had there been no Christmas, there could never have been an Easter. The Eternal Word had to first embrace the humanity of Jesus, live and die as one of us, before he could rise "for us and for our salvation."[178]

But Christmas also makes me mindful of more than the joyous birth of Christ. I grieve the senseless loss of life caused by gun violence. This moral pandemic apparently continues largely unchecked. As worldwide grief, shock, and disbelief mount, the random violence increases exponentially. Disrespect for human life seems to be taken for granted. Such manifest, selfish and wanton evil, now gone global, somehow always raises its ugly head as we approach the beautiful season of Christmas. Why is that? Because amidst the joyful birth of our Savior, we are unable to drown out the dissonance of disrespect that thrives unabated. Such rampant, continuing evil would certainly lead one to wonder about the nature of God, and therefore by logical extension, the nature of Jesus Christ.

In this meditation entitled *Identity* I would like to address precisely who the Babe of Bethlehem *is*, and clearly who He *is*

---

[178] The Nicene Creed.

not. The word *good* is related to the word *God*. How is it then, in light of such rampant, random, unchecked mayhem that has gone on for so long, could anyone honestly use the words *good* and *God* in the same sentence? How can we consider God good, if that God doesn't put an end to evil once and for all? Several questions present themselves around the words *how* and *why*. *How* could a good and loving God permit such tragedy to occur? And *why* would God not have done something by now to prevent it? *Why* were the hearts and minds of perpetrators never converted to sanity and wholeness? And *how* is it that such human beings were never able to hear the human heartbeats of Jesus?

These questions would not appear at face value to qualify as Christmas questions, or do they? They fall within the category of what theologians refer to as *theodicy*, or the *problem of evil*. In my experience, our inability to answer any of the above questions satisfactorily is the chief stumbling block to faith. Unfortunately, theodicy is not widely taught, or at least taught well. The riddle of theodicy must be seen through the lens of another theological principle, that of the *permissive will* of God. The permissive will of God refers to those events which God *allows* to happen. For example, God allows sinful behavior, even though God does not desire or endorse it. Evil events, of whatever description, can *never be willed by God*. Such is logically impossible, given the perfect nature of God. God has endowed humankind with free will with which God will not interfere, except in highly extraordinary circumstances.[179]

Who then *is* Jesus Christ? Who is this Christ Child we adore at Christmas? To answer this adequately, it helps to recall a heresy, a two-faced heresy, both faces of which grossly distort the person of Jesus. We believe that Jesus was

---

179 Miracles, for example, where by divine intervention, the laws of nature are temporarily suspended.

both human *and* divine, both *God* and *man*. But don't take that belief for granted, because it was not always universally accepted. Some misguided theologians insisted that Christ was *only divine*, and not *human* at all. What people encountered on seeing Jesus was only an *apparently* human body, a sham, a trick or phantasm. No *Incarnation* had ever taken place, a divine person taking on human flesh, and therefore there was really nothing to celebrate at Christmas. They claimed Jesus never had a real body like ours, but only *appeared* to have had one. This is the false doctrine of *Docetism*.

Where one heresy crops up, usually its exact opposite will soon surface, hence the two-faced heresy mentioned above. A mirror-image heresy to Docetism denied that Christ was ever at all *divine*. He was arguably a very good guy, another great prophet and superb teacher in the Hebrew tradition, a faith healer too, but no way was he divine. That Jesus Christ was not God was the false doctrine of Arianism. Docetism and Arianism were both wrong because each negated one of the two essential natures of Christ at the expense of the other. They could not accept the dual nature of Christ. Christians believe Jesus was only *one person* but possessing *two natures*, one fully human and the other fully divine. How can two natures coexist within one person? Another *article of faith*, like the Trinity or the real presence of Christ in the Eucharist. You either accept or reject mysteries of faith. You either believe or disbelieve them. They can't be explained, can't be put under a microscope and understood.

God the Creator is a pure spirit,[180] is neither male nor female nor at all human. God's only Son, Jesus Christ, was *quite* human, possessed of a dual nature. He desired to be born the same way we were. He wanted to fully experience

---

180 John 4:24. "God is spirit, and those who worship him must worship in spirit and truth."

the human condition and be able to self-identify as one of us. God went through this exercise on purpose. An angel or some other heavenly flunky could easily have been dispatched to accomplish the work of redemption. But rather than staffing it out, God chose to send God's self in the form of a baby born in poverty.

Throughout the New Testament, we read expressions like "Jesus wept," or "Jesus was moved with pity." We know that he empathized deeply with his sisters and brothers. Countless stories of his compassionate outreach to the fringes of polite society abound in the gospels. In my view, his humanity surpassed all his teaching, preaching, and healing combined. Jesus cared back in the first century and still cares about us in ours. Jesus still stands there beside his fellow human beings weeping at every display of mean-spiritedness. Never giving up on me, Jesus hopes that someday I might finally understand what he was talking about and get it right. But sometimes I just don't listen deeply enough to obey.[181] We are all *subject to evil and death*, and unfortunately, one tragedy tends to spawn the next.

Despite the teachings of the nihilist philosopher Friedrich Nietzsche, I need to remind myself that God is by no means dead. The Babe of Bethlehem is still quite alive and well. Through Jesus, Prince of Peace, God continues to offer humankind a way out. God illumines my pathway to peace when I renounce any support for violence or even for aggression. I pray that we all may sign up for a pilgrimage towards peace. Never giving up, never abandoning hope for a brighter future, let us encourage one another to embrace and hold fast that *perfect love that casts out fear*.[182]

---

[181] The English word "obedience" comes from Latin words meaning "deep listening."

[182] 1 John 4:18.

INTERVIEWS

There's no telling how much folklore has developed around the world regarding felines. But there's one saying which doesn't charm most animal lovers, the maxim suggesting that *curiosity killed the cat*. Well, one would hope for the best, especially if the cat were simply intellectually curious. Curiosity in itself isn't bad. There was a certain kind of Gospel curiosity shown when the Greeks approached one of the apostles saying, "We would like to see Jesus." For the intellectually curious Greek, that meant, "We'd like to interview him, find out what makes him tick."

> Now among those who went up to worship at the festival were some Greeks. They came to Philip, who was from Bethsaida in Galilee, and said to him, "Sir, we wish to see Jesus." Philip went and told Andrew; then Andrew and Philip went and told Jesus.[183]

Some other translations express the request slightly differently: "We would see Jesus" (KJV); "We desire to see Jesus" (AMP); or "We want to meet Jesus" (NLT). Greeks of that era, being non-Jews, would not have enjoyed direct access to Jesus. They would have had to go through Jewish intermediaries to arrange it. Philip, a Jew albeit with a Greek name, seemed a likely person to approach in order to set

---

183 John 12:20-22.

up an interview. Greeks were noted for their learning and intellectual curiosity:

> For since, in the wisdom of God, the world did not know God through wisdom, God decided, through the foolishness of our proclamation, to save those who believe. For Jews demand signs and Greeks desire wisdom, but we proclaim Christ crucified, a stumbling block to Jews and foolishness to Gentiles, but to those who are the called, both Jews and Greeks, Christ the power of God and the wisdom of God.[184]

How can we fault such cultured Greek gentlemen for wanting to encounter Jesus? We have to assume they were on their own sincere spiritual path. We cannot assume they planned to fire off a series of gotcha questions. After all, they had journeyed all that distance for the Passover celebration. They had gone through proper channels, making appropriate contact to arrange an interview. And so, Jesus had been duly informed of the request, but there was to be no interview. Jesus listens to their request as relayed by Philip and Andrew and simply proceeds to ignore it. He does not pick up at all on what his disciples were reporting. This time oddly enough he doesn't make an exception and consent to minister outside his immediate flock. Actually, he doesn't say yes and he doesn't say no. He just takes the conversation in a wholly different direction. Simply put, at this point in his life, Jesus has precious little time for interviews, for intellectually inclined curiosity seekers or even for mildly interested inquirers. Time is short. He needs to concentrate on the basics. He feels obligated to teach the essentials of the

---

184 1 Corinthians 1:21-24.

faith rather than debate cerebral matters of philosophical theology.

Once again, Jesus reveals what is about to happen to him, this time through a simple gardening lesson. A seed must be planted, die, and decompose before any new growth may emerge. He reiterates the essential Gospel lesson, the paradox about preserving life as you now know it versus forfeiting it in favor of the larger life:

> Those who love their life lose it, and those who hate their life in this world will keep it for eternal life.[185]

Jesus is literally coming to a *crucial* moment, his moment of the *crux*, the cross. He has no time to waste with small talk. This is no moment for Jesus to escape his vulnerable humanity. He is scared, as well he should be. With a slightly shaky voice he slowly pronounces these words:

> Now my soul is troubled. And what should I say—'Father, save me from this hour'? No, it is for this reason that I have come to this hour.[186]

All human trepidation aside, his *divine mission* must override any aspect of his *human safety*:

> In the days of his flesh, Jesus offered up prayers and supplications, with loud cries and tears, to the one who was able to save him from death, and he was heard because of his reverent submission.[187]

---

185 John 12:29.
186 John 12:17.
187 Hebrews 5:7.

Jesus must *live out* his own Gospel paradox. Essentially, he must *hate* his earthly life, *renounce* life as he knows it that others may embrace eternal life. It's both that simple and that challenging. Twelve-step recovery literature suggests that working the program is *simple* but not *easy*. Jesus himself would have probably shouted a loud Aramaic *Amen* to that gem of wisdom.

Do you ever wonder where the conversation might have gone, had the Greeks ever gotten their audience with Jesus? What might they have asked Jesus about? What would they have wanted to discuss? Might their hearts have been opened to hear the Gospel paradox? They were inquirers, seekers potentially interested in *The Way*, that new sect of Judaism which we later would call *Christianity*. But were they emotionally prepared for the hard sayings of Jesus, the harsh realities, and crucial words the Savior was about to utter? What if we had been there? How would you or I have reacted, had we asked for and been granted an interview?

In the life of Christ, these scriptures occur right before Holy Week. As his passion and death approached, Jesus would engage in less and less small talk, a minimum of unnecessary speech. Perhaps this was primarily why he ignored the Greeks' request for an interview. How might I emulate more sparse speech myself? Perhaps this next Lent I might fast and abstain from chat rooms, Instagram reading, Facebooking, instant messaging, tweeting, and the like. Am I willing and able essentially to absent myself from trivial pursuits for the sake of silence? What matters *really* matter? What habits might better promote a profitable season of Lent?

It must have been a somber experience for Jesus to contemplate his execution but hours ahead. And often we as well find ourselves gripped with fear as we face an uncertain future. Only with God's grace surrounding us are we able to face it. The third and fourth stanzas of one hymn[188] encourage us to

> Come, labor on!
> Away with gloomy doubts and faithless fear!
> No arm so weak but may do service here:
> By feeblest agents may our God fulfill
> His righteous will.
>
> Come, labor on!
> Claim the high calling angels cannot share—
> To young and old the Gospel gladness bear;
> Redeem the time; its hours too swiftly fly.
> The night draws nigh.

When I have questions, I pray that I may have the courage to request my own private interview with Jesus. I am confident that such an interview will be readily granted. I want to be energized to "bear the Gospel gladness to young and old." May I firmly resist any temptation to sugar-coat or water down the Gospel paradox, as I wait in joyful hope for Resurrection Life!

---

188 *Hymnal 1982*, #541.

Joy

When I was a teenager, we attended a little parish church in New York State right over the Connecticut border. We did so, because the pastor happened to be my uncle's seminary classmate. So, rather than attending a local Connecticut parish, we chose one across the state line. Although we were card-carrying Roman Catholics, purportedly respectful of church rules about observing parish boundaries, well, as far as that went, my Mom behaved more like a practicing Episcopalian than an observant Roman Catholic. Wherever we lived, we'd attend the parish Mom picked out, irrespective of parish boundaries. Mom had very good taste, I must admit. A very cultured palate for good liturgy.

Well, the pastor at St. Patrick's, Bedford Village was elevated to the rank of Monsignor and thus got to wear robes like an Episcopal Dean or Canon. Choir dress for such a minor prelate includes cassock with red buttons and piping, a scarlet fascia[189] with a red pom on the biretta. The next Sunday this newly-minted Monsignor went to the pulpit he quipped, "Well, folks, now I'm in the red more ways than one!" That zinger I'll never forget. Beside the hilarity he made a thoughtful observation: red can signify either debt or distinction.

Colors do send signals. Ask any fashionista. Before

---

[189] Sash.

inclusive language came of age, we would say "Clothes make the man." But German always said, "Clothes make people."[190] There's a lot of truth in that. Another maxim advises one to "dress for success." Wearing red, for example, is considered wearing a *power* color. And, if you think about the fastidious liturgical vesture on display in certain, well-heeled parishes, you might begin to wonder.

In any case, when you attend Mass in mid-Advent or mid-Lent, you very likely won't see the customary violet vestments. Those two Sundays the church gives you an option to be "in the pink." Parishes willing to purchase a complete set of rose vestments for use only two Sundays of the year are making a statement. But of more significance, why are rose-colored vestments used on these Sundays? Related to this question is another: why during Advent is the third candle on the Advent wreath also pink? What's with the rose? Why in the pink?

While no one would seriously deny the proverb that clothes "make" people, liturgical vesture is not supposed to make a fashion statement. Choice of vestment color was never intended to be at the whim of the celebrant. It is mandated by the liturgical season or feast day. Once when I was an altar server, I remember an unusual St. Patrick's Day when the celebrant chose green vestments instead of white. His Irish fashion statement taste didn't even stop there. He also instructed the organist to play "Danny Boy" as a prelude to Mass! At the Offertory, I was relieved to discover that the altar wine was still red. This little vignette might have been dubbed "Priests Gone Wild." While entertaining in the moment, this priest's bad behavior makes a point: liturgical colors convey meaning. Liturgy is scripted never improv. And assigned colors always signify something.

---

190 *Kleider machen Leute.*

The Third Sunday of Advent is a *Rose* Sunday, sometimes called *Rejoice*[191] or *Refreshment* Sunday. The usual liturgical colors for Advent are blue or violet, rather somber symbols setting a more introspective tone. Rose, permitted only on the third Sunday, purposely conveys a more joyful, upbeat mood than blue or purple. Half-way through Advent, we are invited to look up, to pause from inward introspection. The Church invites a smile rather than a frown as we anticipate Jesus' imminent arrival. Rose Sunday manages to hit the pause button during Advent. We temporarily turn away from introspection toward anticipation. Jesus is on the way and, amidst all our soul-searching, we need to recall that. And it doesn't take much soul-searching to pick up on the word *rejoice* sprinkled all throughout Rose Sunday's readings. The pink paraments of the day all but shout-out the word: REJOICE!

Which scriptures call us to *rejoice* on mid-Advent Sunday? What might these words have to say to us? Isaiah suggests we make use of "the oil of gladness instead of [that of] mourning" and that we don "the mantle of praise instead of [that of] a faint spirit."[192] He continues encouraging us to embrace a positive frame of mind when he proclaims:

> I will greatly rejoice in the LORD, my
> whole being shall exult in my God; for
> he has clothed me with the garments of
> salvation, he has covered me with the
> robe of righteousness.[193]

One Advent collect goes so far as to exhort us to change our clothes:

---

191 Also referred to as *Gaudete* Sunday, from the first word of the original Latin liturgy meaning "rejoice."
192 Isaiah 61:3.
193 Isaiah 61:10.

> Let us take off the works of darkness and
> put on the armor of light.[194]

The first action we are to undertake is essentially to "rip off and toss into the nearest dumpster" the flimsy, filthy, threadbare rags of darkness; and the second thing for us to do is "respectfully and with great dignity, dress and vest ourselves" in the armor-like clothing of light.

The toxic waste in our lives, *the works of darkness*, usually cause the pronounced absence of joy. That feeling of being down and discouraged persists and we don't know why. To emerge from that depression, we are advised to discard our metaphorical mantle of darkness and intentionally re-invest in sturdier, spiritual clothing. The color conveyed by Rose Sunday asks us to arm ourselves with the vesture of joy and thereby with the power to rejoice. Di-vesting and re-investing suggests bold imagery. Is not this the very work of Advent, discarding darkness to embrace light, exchanging purple for pink, and the faint spirit of mournfulness for the robust robe of rejoicing? One psalm says as much:

> Then was our mouth filled with laughter,
> and our tongue with shouts of joy.
>
> Those who sowed with tears will reap with
> songs of joy.[195]

In the anticipation of Christmas, no words could be more joyful than those of the *Magnificat*, as Mary exclaims:

> My soul proclaims the greatness of
> the Lord, my spirit rejoices in God my
> Savior.[196]

---

[194] Romans 13:12. Vulgate: *Abjiciamus* ergo opera tenebrarum; et *induamur* arma lucis.
[195] Psalm 126:2, 6.
[196] Luke 1:46.

And lest we might still harbor doubts about maintaining a genuinely rosy outlook on life, Paul encourages us to:

> Rejoice in the Lord always; again, I will say, Rejoice. Let your gentleness be known to everyone. The Lord is near. Do not worry about anything...[197]

Rejoice Sunday reinforces God's desire that Christians be positive, optimistic, forward-looking, and hopeful. We need to quit peeking in the rear-view mirror, reliving, relitigating the slings and arrows of our past. Every Advent God reminds us to make better use of our time. Quit looking down, focus forward not backward, picturing ourselves already "in the pink." That's not gawking at pie in the sky. That's greeting holy water from heaven.

---

[197] Philippians 4:4.

KNOWLEDGE

Bible quotes and book titles sometimes seem to say it all. Some are so clever, so on the mark and to the point that their meaning jumps out at you. You might even skip reading the whole bible passage or the entire book. Those few well-chosen words tell all. They say, you can't tell a book *by its cover*, but occasionally you can *by its title*. An example would be a book entitled *Thoughts Matter*.[198] You can even skip the subtitle.

Bible quotes of that ilk are often found in epistles. One is so transparent that it qualifies as one of those "quotable quotes" you find in *Readers' Digest*. Paul comments on whether Christians should ever to partake of the ceremonial food offered to idols:

> Now concerning food sacrificed to idols: we know that "all of us possess knowledge." Knowledge puffs up, but love builds up. Anyone who claims to know something does not yet have the necessary knowledge; but anyone who loves God is known by him.[199]

Actually, this passage starts off talking about something completely foreign if not meaningless to us today. Nowadays,

---

198 *Thoughts Matter: The Practice of Spiritual Life* by Sister Mary Margaret Funke (New York: Continuum, 2006).

199 1 Corinthians 8:1-3.

at least in our culture, eating food offered to idols is pretty much a non-issue. Upon hearing "food sacrificed to idols," I might at first be tempted to tune out and check my smartphone. But as I listen further, I discover the *real* message is not about food at all. It's about knowledge and love, and how we deal with both. The golden nugget of Paul's teaching appears in the next sentence:

> Knowledge puffs up, but love builds up.[200]

This is the real point of this passage. The Latin Vulgate expresses this thought using cognates with familiar English words which facilitate our understanding of Paul's meaning:

> Scientia inflat; caritas vero aedificat.

Knowledge *inflates* us, blows us up, pumps a lot of hot air into us. But love, on the other hand, *edifies*, builds us up, creates new living spaces within us. Misapplied knowledge amounts to no more than hot air. There is, of course, nothing *per se* intrinsically wrong with knowledge. It is obviously good and we need it. But to apply it unwisely or injudiciously is to degrade it to a level that equates with blowing hot air. In this particular passage, Paul was teaching about avoiding even the *possibility* of giving scandal, even an *appearance* of impropriety. He was not holding forth about fine dining. While there was nothing sinful in and of itself to eat food offered to idols, onlookers might have misconstrued what they saw, thinking that Christians were actively participating in idol worship. Therefore, the more prudent practice would be to eat something else somewhere else, lest confusion be sown by those known as followers of the *Way*.[201]

---

200 1 Corinthians 8:1.
201 The term *The Way* was that which the early Christians used to describe their newfound expression of faith.

Ah, knowledge and love, the head and the heart: the cognitive and the affective components of our human nature. Both aspects are complementary and essential to our human nature. The New Testament, however, emphasizes that *to love* is more important than *to know*. Or as the proverb puts it, a*mor vincit omnia.*[202] While I can't claim to remember much from my theology classes, there is one encounter I do remember from a course in sacramental theology. Mastering the scrupulous detail associated with each of the seven sacraments was daunting, if not simply over the top. Lost in the labyrinthine detail of minutiae surrounding one of the sacraments, one day our professor simply stopped lecturing and said: "Guys, just remember this: there are probably a lot of theologians in hell." After the anticipated raucous laughter had subsided, this needful moment of comic relief made us all realize a deeper truth. K*nowledge*—no matter how much of it—was not going to determine whether we were to go upstairs or downstairs after death. The deciding factor would be based, at least in part, on how we *applied* our knowledge: were we legalists or did we love?

Paul was advising the Corinthians to forgo food for idols, even though it was *legal* to consume it. He urged them not to indulge because that was the more *loving* thing to do. Otherwise, some observers might misinterpret why the fledgling Christians were doing so. Once again, apparent conflict arises between what is *legal* and what is *moral*. We could go into that at great length, and frankly I'd like to, but that would take us far afield of this meditation.

We find a similar situation when Jesus encounters the temple establishment.[203] During a routine Sabbath service, Jesus heals a man with an unclean spirit. The extent of the

---

202 Love conquers all.
203 Matthew 7:28-29; Mark 1: 21-28; Luke 4:31-37.

man's demonic possession was highlighted when the demons spoke and referred to themselves in the plural (*we/us*). This poor fellow was seriously stricken. This was no head cold. Jesus directly addressed the multiple demonic powers and the man emerged totally healed. But how did the worshipers of Jesus' day receive this? How did they process what they had just witnessed?

> They were all amazed, and they kept on asking one another, "What is this? A new teaching—with authority! He commands even the unclean spirits, and they obey him."[204]

They could only interpret Jesus' actions as a demonstration of his *authority*. They were unable to recognize that he was primarily motivated to heal out of *love*. For this audience, such a novel point of view was a new revelation. But Jesus was much more focused on *loving* someone to wholeness rather than on simply revealing his divine identity. The majority population of Jesus' time were not yet equipped to embrace the primacy of love. They literally couldn't get their arms around it. They were stuck in a unidimensional, cognitive view of their reality. They could not contemplate assimilating anything beyond intellectual learning. They could not realize that everything Jesus did was because he cared so deeply. They could not fathom a heart moved to heal rather than to instruct. They were unable to recognize that Jesus' healing acts were solely motivated by love. He had no need to show off his divine power or impress others. From this point on in the life of Christ, the reigning religious establishment began to dig in their heels and insist on law over spirit, knowledge over love, and head over heart.

---

204 Mark 1:27-28.

And so, where does this leave us who contemplate this teaching today? Certainly with some serious soul-searching to do. Where would I stand, for example, were I present to this temple scenario? Would I have been able then to identify with Jesus' first impulse to love by healing? Or might I have remained a first century skeptic, trapped in a physical rather than transported into the metaphysical framework of reality? Do I have sufficient room in my life to account for mystery, to embrace miracles? Does everything for me have to be quantifiable, cut-and-dried, and straightforward? What growing edge might there be for me to grow in my life in the Spirit? Perhaps neither of us can adequately address these questions right now, but I want to raise them anyway. May at least some of these ruminations provide the grist for fruitful meditation along our earthly pilgrimage. God the Holy Spirit, the Paraclete, will by definition be one to *walk beside us* and gradually and graciously to *lead us into all truth*.

LEAVE

Opening collects are a treasure trove of spiritual gems. Their purpose is to introduce the liturgical theme, sounding as it were the leitmotiv. One such prayer refers to "our unruly wills and affections," admitting that only God can bring them into order:

> Almighty God, you alone can bring into order the unruly wills and affections of sinners: Grant your people grace to love what you command and desire what you promise; that, among the swift and varied changes of the world,[205] our hearts may surely there be fixed where true joys are to be found.[206]

Unruly is such a wonderfully descriptive word meaning *without rules* or *lacking order*, or in other words, describing something or someone without proper boundaries. In that collect, we admit that our will and affections, what we want and how we feel, are often misaligned with our best selves. Moreover, we acknowledge that we're caught up in the *swift and varied changes of the world*, life's vicissitudes, which inhibit a proper focus of one's will and one's affections. This prayer asks God for the virtue of stability, the steadiness to handle whatever *rapid and unforeseen events* might confront

---

205 *BCP 1979*, p. 167 (traditional) "among the sundry and manifold changes of the world."
206 *BCP 1979*, p. 219 (contemporary).

us, as we anticipate a reversal of the psalmist's words about beginning in sorrow and ending in joy:

> Those who sowed with tears will reap with songs of joy. Those who go out weeping, carrying the seed, will come again with joy, shouldering their sheaves.[207]

Sometimes, it just doesn't work that way. Sometimes, life just goes in reverse. We might have put it differently. Since we are subject to the *swift and varied changes of the world*, is it not more likely that we begin with joy and end in sorrow? Is the following not a more accurate version of life as we know it?

> Those who sowed with songs of joy will reap with tears of sorrow. Those who go out with joy, shouldering their sheaves, carrying the seed, will return home weeping with regret.

What could possibly bring about such an unfortunate turn of events, such a cruel reversal of fate? Isn't it always better to move from negative to positive rather than the other way around? About a week before the Last Supper, Jesus stops off at the home of his best friends, Lazarus, Martha, and Mary. Bethany was his home away from home. Just recently, at the healing hands of Jesus Lazarus had come back to life, certainly a move in a positive direction. Martha was the activist, doer, cook, hostess, organizer, and all-around go-to person. Mary the mystic was just the opposite, happy to be sitting at Jesus' feet contemplating his real presence. On this visit, perhaps his last, Mary wanted to perform an act of special devotion for Jesus. She anointed him using *a pound of*

---

207 Psalm 126:6-7.

costly perfume made of pure nard, whose distinct fragrance filled the entire house.[208] That well-intentioned, positive gesture was also highly symbolic, since for Jesus, the next time would be his last, when he would be anointed with myrrh as his burial spice. Mary, who worshiped and adored Jesus, was intuitively performing Jesus' burial ritual in advance.

But due to the unholy presence of Judas Iscariot, this ritual would turn from positive to negative, because someone would take Mary's holy anointing in the opposite direction. He would criticize her for her extravagance in using all this costly fragrance on one person at one sitting, thereby perverting Mary's beautiful gesture into ugly wastefulness:

> "Why was this perfume not sold for three hundred denarii and the money given to the poor?" (He said this not because he cared about the poor, but because he was a thief; he kept the common purse and used to steal what was put into it.)[209]

Judas' attitude is so egregious that even the Gospel writer feels compelled to explain his bad behavior. John seeks to interpret why Judas would hijack goodness and take it in the opposite direction, perverting good to look like evil. Jesus, just as directly as he confronted the devil in the desert, chastises Judas sternly:

> Jesus said, "Leave her alone. She bought it so that she might keep it for the day of my burial. You always have the poor with you, but you do not always have me."[210]

A direct rebuff to the soon-to-be traitor: "Leave her

---

208 John 12:3.
209 John 12:5-6.
210 John 12:7-8.

alone," pretty strong language for Jesus, but very much to the point. Jesus tells Judas the truth, pointing to the death that would befall him because of this erstwhile apostle's greed. The sudden appearance of Judas Iscariot at an intimate dinner among close friends—Jesus, Lazarus, Martha, and Mary—remains unexplained. But could we not chalk that up as well to the *swift and varied changes of the world,* the *rapid and unforeseen events* that often arise? Judas appeared unexpectedly, hurriedly, and without warning. His showing up was unforeseen. Maybe he had been stalking Jesus, who knows? But Jesus' words neutralized the venom Judas had planned to inject. It is often very hard if not altogether impossible to be prepared for a sudden turn of events. While out on the water on a pleasant sunny day, a squall can come out of nowhere, sending sailors scrambling to keep the ship afloat.

"Keeping the ship afloat" might serve as an apt metaphor for this meditation. When I start out joyfully and suddenly find myself assaulted by sorrow, I will surely need God's help to keep my spiritual life afloat. The collect claims that "God alone is able to bring into order the unruly wills and affections" of those who would take us in the wrong direction. Only Jesus can issue such an order as, *Leave her alone!* I need him to tell that to the forces of evil when they show up uninvited. He will issue the same order on our behalf: *Leave them alone, get lost!* May our Lord always help us redirect our wills and affections toward goodness and joy, light and life.

LIBERATION

The first stanza of a well-known hymn addresses the issue of liberating people from spiritual and emotional darkness:

> Come, thou long expected Jesus,
> Born to set thy people free;
> From our sins and fears release us,
> Let us find our rest in thee.[211]

And there is a collect which likewise prays for the freedom from darkness to embrace life:

> Set us free, O God,
> from the bondage of our sins,
> and give us the liberty of that abundant life
> which you have made known to us
> in your Son, our Savior Jesus Christ.[212]

The expectation of both hymn and collect is that we need to be set free, released from the bondage of all that is dark in exchange for *the liberty of abundant life*. We are asking God to free us from whatever shackles are preventing our freedom of movement in a positive direction. We confess that right now we feel stymied, caught like a trapped animal. We see no possible way to self-extricate from the cold metallic

---

211 *Hymnal 1982* # 66.
212 *BCP 1979*, p. 216: Collect for the Fifth Sunday after Epiphany.

vise holding us captive. Into such an apparently hopeless situation we call out to *Yeshua ha-Mashiach*,[213] asking for two graces, two special favors. We first ask him to come release us from what is trapping us. But that's not all. We also need our freedom to embrace the *more abundant life*[214] that only the Messiah can deliver. St. John doesn't quote Jesus as saying "I have come to bring you [just plain ordinary] abundant life," but rather "an *even more* abundant life," one fuller than you could ever have imagined! The gospel writer intentionally uses the comparative adverb *abundantius*, more abundantly. This semantic upgrade is a fine-point nuance often missed in Bible translations. Here Jesus is not talking about *ordinary* but *extraordinary* life, the kind only he can offer.

Fears, sins, and the bondage of sin are daily realities. These spiritual impediments trap us, and we need to be freed. In the Lord's Prayer we pray, "Give us today our daily bread." A parallel prayer might be, "Deliver us today from our daily bondage to spiritual warfare, sickness, and death." In order to ingest the sustenance we ask for, such liberation is essential. Jesus was moved to heal one very sick man with multiple physical as well as spiritual health issues. Jesus released this chronically ill individual and set him free, but not just to wander off weak and wounded. No, Jesus restored him to that *more abundant life* modeled in the life of Christ.

Paul provides some practical wisdom how we can help heal one another within the Body of Christ, the Church. He shows how we might follow in Jesus' footsteps to share that more abundant life with others. Too often, we are "Johnny one notes" on the piano of life. We have our own tried-and-true way of relating to other people, or at least so we think.

---

213 *Yeshua ha-Mashiach* (הישׁוּע המשׁיח) means Jesus the Messiah.
214 John 10:10. "I am come that they might have life, and that they might have it more abundantly." (KJV); "Ego veni ut vitam habeant, et abundantius habeant." (Vulgate).

But in ministering to others, one size definitely does not fit all. "Off-the-rack" responses to our siblings seeking health, healing, and wholeness won't cut it. Pat phrases and worn-out cliches cannot address the injuries inflicted by the slings and arrows of an often outrageous world. Paul expressed his methodology of mission this way:

> I have become all things to all people,
> that I might by all means save some. I do
> it all for the sake of the gospel, so that I
> may share in its blessings.[215]

"For the sake of the gospel." For the sake of bringing good news to all sorts and conditions of men and women. You simply can't accomplish that by using a broad-brush approach. We can't send everybody on our social media friends list the same instant message. Each person needs to be addressed on whatever particular frequency they can receive. Paul didn't dream that up all by himself. He learned that technique by imitating Christ. Jesus relates to each human being as an individual. When you communicate in someone else's native language, they can hear you because they are listening with *the ear of the heart*.[216] The miracle of Pentecost is not frozen in time millennia ago but is repeated over and over again throughout human history:

> All of them were filled with the Holy Spirit
> and began to speak in other languages,
> as the Spirit gave them ability. Now there
> were devout Jews from every nation
> under heaven living in Jerusalem. And at
> this sound the crowd gathered and was
> bewildered, because each one heard them

---

215 1 Corinthians 9:22.
216 *Rule of Benedict*, Prologue 1: *Inclina aurem cordis tui*.

> speaking in their own native language.
> In our own languages we hear them
> speaking about God's deeds of power."[217]

The miracle of Pentecost was one of effective communication, employing language tailored to individuals not the masses. This model of one-on-one communication is discipleship at its best.

Is my life already abundant? How could it become slightly more abundant? Do I regularly encounter people, even including family or close friends, who don't catch my drift? Do I sometimes feel like I'm shouting down the proverbial rain barrel when I talk about spiritual things? How could I communicate more effectively with people I meet and perhaps thus influence them for the better? Who are the people in my orbit with whom I might share the Good News that Jesus heals? It's always a good time to ask the Holy Spirit for the gift of tongues[218] properly understood, not as some improv display of gibberish or nonsensical noise. The miracle of the gift of tongues enables us to speak so that others may hear. Small wonder that the words *hearing* and *healing* only differ by one letter.

---

[217] Acts 2:4-6, 11.
[218] Acts 2:3-4.

LIFE

Almighty God, you alone can bring into order the unruly wills and affections of sinners: Grant your people grace to love what you command and desire what you promise; that, among the swift and varied changes of the world, our hearts may surely there be fixed where true joys are to be found.[219]

More often than not, the opening collect at Mass is over and done with so fast that we hardly pay it much more than passing attention. Yet those prayers are composed to sound the leitmotiv of the scriptures that follow. This collect acknowledges that God alone is able to straighten out *our unruly wills and affections*. And what might those be? The first thing I think of when I hear the word *unruly* is a "bad hair day," that wild, messy, unkempt look, the very antithesis of neatness and good order. Literally, the word *unruly* means *without rules* or *lacking order*, or in other words, lacking appropriate boundaries. We are admitting in this collect that more often than not our *wills and affections*, what we want and how we feel, often do not represent our best selves.

Furthermore, we admit we are caught up in the *swift and varied changes of the world*, those vicissitudes of life which inhibit us from appropriately focusing either our wills or our affections. This prayer petitions God for *stability, constancy,*

---

[219] *BCP 1979*, p. 219.

and *steadiness* amidst whatever rapid unforeseen events the world might throw at us. Within such an arena of combat we can see at least two scriptural challenges. One is found in Hebrew Scripture and the other in the Gospel. Though stemming from two distinct sources, the two are not unrelated. Though originating in different contexts, each coaxes forth life from death. The basic message, however, is the same: God can and will always desire to bring life out of death.

In the Hebrew scripture about dry bones,[220] the Lord draws the prophet into dialog and poses a simple question:

> The hand of the Lord came upon me, and he brought me out by the spirit of the Lord and set me down in the middle of a valley; it was full of bones. He led me all around them; there were very many lying in the valley, and they were very dry. He said to me, "Mortal, can these bones live?" I answered, "O Lord God, you know."[221]

Ezekiel's answer "You know" was shorthand for "You know you can, Lord. You know you can make anything live again, Lord, even though those bones *appear* totally dry, totally beyond ever living again." The Lord then instructs Ezekiel to perform his ministry by prophesying, sending various messages to these dry bones, promising that God wills that they should no longer stay dry but come back to life.

> Then he said to me, "Prophesy to these bones, and say to them: O dry bones, hear the word of the Lord. Thus says the Lord

---

[220] Ezekiel 37:1-14.
[221] Ezekiel 37:1-3.

God to these bones: I will cause breath to enter you, and you shall live. I will lay sinews on you, and will cause flesh to come upon you, and cover you with skin, and put breath in you, and you shall live; and you shall know that I am the Lord."[222]

Ezekiel obeyed, and it worked: out of death came life. Living waters began to flow in what had previously been a hopelessly barren desert.

John's Gospel encounter surrounding the death of Lazarus[223] opens another window into God's ability to restore life. While Ezekiel devotes only thirteen verses to his story, John provides over three times that many, thereby supplying a much richer context. Bethany is well-known as Jesus' home away from home. That's where he went to kick back, have a gin and tonic, put his feet up, rest from the heat of the day, and get a good night's rest. His closest friends who lived there were a brother and his two sisters: Lazarus, Martha, and Mary. The two sisters are generally well-known, one a mystic, the other a worker bee. Most are familiar with their differing personality types: Mary the contemplative and Martha the activist.

What had just transpired in their household was totally traumatic for both sisters. The man of the house, their only brother Lazarus, had just died suddenly. The Bible supplies no further details. He just died and his sisters were bereft. They called for their closest family friend, Jesus. He was some distance away, heard about it, but didn't come right away. Given his close relationship with the three, everyone had expected Jesus would rush there immediately. Both sisters believed that if Jesus had been there, Lazarus would never

---

222 Ezekiel 37: 4-6.
223 John 11:1-45.

have died in the first place. But Jesus hadn't been close nearby when it happened. He was quite a distance away and upon hearing the news didn't travel back immediately. At first glance, this would look bad, but there are reasons why Jesus didn't rush back right way. In my view, the most plausible reason is that Jesus didn't really need to be there immediately. God's healing presence is not restricted to physical *chronos* (clock time) but operates rather on metaphysical *kairos*, (eternal time). God does not perform miracles on our timetable but on quite another. Jesus could and in fact did heal Lazarus without respect to either distance or time. On Jesus' return, Lazarus was quickly brought back to life, and for all we know, lived to enjoy a good long one.

How can I come to terms with my own dry bones ever being restored to life? How can what I consider to be an apparent corpse come back from the grave? More to the point, how do I look at *Life after Life*? A book by that very clever title in fact first appeared in 1975.[224] In that pioneering work, a medical doctor documented over a hundred near-death experiences revealing their stunning consistency with one another.[225] But *Life after Life* is far more than a catchy book title. It is in fact the core doctrine we enunciate at every Requiem Mass: "for to your faithful servants, O Lord, life is

---

224 The groundbreaking, bestselling classic, *Life After Life*, is now available in a special fortieth-anniversary edition that includes a new Foreword from Eben Alexander, M.D., author of *Proof of Heaven*, and a new Afterword by the author.

225 With his book *Life After Life*, Raymond Moody, M.D. launched the modern NDE (Near Death Experience) movement which revolutionized how we think about death and the hereafter. His study reported on over a hundred patients who had experienced "clinical death" and were revived. Each participant recounted in their own words what lies beyond the flatline. A bestseller of over thirteen million copies, *Life After Life* introduced concepts including the bright light, the tunnel, and the encouraging presence of loved ones waiting on the other side, all now much better understood today. His was the catalyst that paved the way for other publications which reshaped our notions about life and death.

changed not ended." Theologically speaking, the common phrase *life after death* is therefore inaccurate. Dr. Moody properly reworded that phrase for us as *life after life*.

Neither dry bones nor rotting corpses can claim exemption from the healing power of Jesus. Neither are excluded from Resurrection life. If we listen carefully, we can hear an echo of the leitmotiv from *Rejoice Sunday*. Whatever valleys of death we may face ahead, Jesus wants to reassure us how the story will end. He will be that welcoming figure of light at the end of the tunnel as we enter life after life. Someday I'll be called to go through that tunnel. But whenever that is, I'll be looking for the light, the *lux perfecta*[226] at the end of my tunnel, the gateway to glory.

---

226 Perfect Light, the *lumen Christi*, the light of Christ.

LIGHT

Remember Christmas cards? Of late, most holiday greetings arrive via email. Whether it's the cost of the cards, higher postal rates or just the immediacy and convenience of Internet communication, sending Christmas greetings by snail mail has largely gone out of fashion. "Real" Christmas cards accompanied by an annual letter are at risk of becoming an endangered species. Two real Christmas cards I recently received, however, did catch my attention and are worthy of comment. One came from a seminary dean. His brief and succinct message began with a Gospel verse:

> The light shines in the darkness, And the darkness has not overcome it.[227]

to which he appended his own verse:

> but not for lack of trying.

Wow! "But not for lack of trying." Cynical, but given the historical period in which he was adding that snarky comment, probably on target. However, he then restated the positive and hopeful words of the Gospel once again:

> The light shines in the darkness, And the darkness has not overcome it.

---

[227] John 1:5 (NIV).

His card concluded with a prayer that

> "In this holy season,
> Let us be friends of the light:
> Those who bear it
> And those who seek it."

How hard has darkness ever tried to *overcome* the light in your life? I often find it helpful to recall the message of a certain collect and recite it whenever darkness threatens to approach, when I am tempted to give in to it rather than seek the light:

> Almighty God, give us grace
> to cast away the works of darkness,
> and put on the armor of light.[228]

Where was the seminary dean going with his Christmas letter? What do I get when I try to connect the dots, to read between the lines? There are some obvious answers. Seldom does a *single* source of evil block anyone's light. Don't forget the old adage that "all [good] things come in threes." The word *good* is bracketed because unfortunately those triads are not all necessarily *good*. And also, whatever might come our way, for good or for ill, often goes well beyond three. Do you remember Jesus' conversation with the fellow believed to be demon-possessed?

> Jesus then asked him, "What is your
> name?" He said, "Legion"; for many
> demons had entered him.[229]

There are admittedly *many demons*, whether in nature, politics or humankind. All qualify as demons. The more evil

---
228 Collect for the First Sunday in Advent.
229 Luke 8:30.

they are, the more the light gets blocked and the more our vision is impaired. Another friend of mine enclosed a poem with his Christmas card. It was entitled "Welcome, New Year," followed by three exclamation points. His sentiments are similar to those of the dean. His poem though, while realistic, remains optimistic. He yearns to begin again, to make a fresh start, without normalizing or minimizing what has transpired over the past year:

Welcome, New Year!!!

> The sun, thoroughly embarrassed, moves southward.
> Twelve months of its brilliant light has brought little benefit.
> And so, the Reign of Light is now abdicating:
> Darkness amplifying, Greed abounding
> Honesty abating, Truth acquiescing.
> Such a season of gathering gloom strains to herald
> The faint glow of a Dawn approaching,
> The amber rays of Hope struggling to birth.

His frank appraisal of a bleaker past is softened by his hope for a brighter future:

> May the New Year bring our weary world
> The welcome gifts of
> Truth, Compassion, and Peace.

I do love Christmas. It has always brought me the greatest happiness of any season of the year. Had there been no

Christmas, there would have been no Easter. Jesus insisted on condescending, on literally "coming down," joining humankind and living among us mere mortals, before he would die and rise again *for us and for our salvation*.[230] Christmas should always be a season of unparalleled, unmitigated joy. History, however, continues to baffle us with the confusing cognitive dissonance between darkness and light. The weak flame of light flickering in our world seems subject to extinction by one darkness after another. Such a challenge calls us to a special category of mindfulness. We must be ever mindful of *this fragile earth, our island home*.[231] Devastating fires, ongoing drought, virtually unchecked gun violence, manifest disregard for human life, and political perfidy seem at times all but unstoppable. When such manifold darkness descends locally as well as globally, our vision becomes clouded to the point of virtual blindness. My friend did not ask the question, but I will:

Where is GOD in all this? Where IS God when all this is happening?

The rampant, persistent, unchecked darkness on our planet calls the question about the nature of God. The obvious "elephant-in-the-room" question is, where is Jesus when all this darkness descends? How do we deal with this most unwelcome elephant? Or, to put the question yet another way,

Who *is* the Son of God and who *is* he *not*?

Surrounded, enveloped by so much darkness we dare not forget a core, non-negotiable principle of our theology: whenever or wherever evil takes place, that evil can never in any way, shape or form ever be *God's will*. We must internalize that truth, the logical impossibility for God ever to will evil.

---

230 The Nicene Creed.
231 *BCP 1979*, Eucharistic Prayer C, p. 370.

Another core, non-negotiable principle of our theology is that Jesus of Nazareth is both God and man. The *Incarnation* means that the divinity of God took on an additional element: the flesh and blood of an ordinary human being. Divinity both adopted and assimilated humanity. The New Testament frequently reports that *Jesus wept* or that he was *moved with pity*. The God-man cared deeply about his fellow human beings. Countless stories abound attesting to Jesus' apparently inexhaustible compassion for people, his empathetic embrace especially of those whom everyone else had sidelined. It would be no exaggeration that Jesus' humanity surpassed all his other gifts of teaching, preaching, and healing combined. Jesus cared back then and continues to care right now very deeply for all of us and about all of us. Jesus stands right there next to us in our every darkness, weeping alongside us. Jesus is right there beside us witnessing every display of violence, every dealing of injustice, and every nonsensical denial of obvious truth. Jesus weeps once more. But I need to remember that the Christ Child I have come to love so deeply at his Christmas creche will never give up on me, never stop hoping that someday I'll make better choices. Jesus weeps, yes, but Jesus also hopes.

But so often I just don't listen, don't sense his real presence when he's standing right there next to me. Eucharistic Prayer A cautions that we are "subject to evil and death."[232] One tragedy spawns another and there we are again caught in that cycle of evil which leads to death. Regardless what the nihilist philosopher Friedrich Nietzsche taught, God is *not* dead. Not at all. By no means. Not by any stretch of the imagination. On the contrary, God is very much alive and well. Through the life and ministry of Jesus, humankind has been offered an alternative way, the pathway to peace and ultimately to

---

[232] *BCP 1979*, p. 362.

a non-violent society, one that embraces the helpless and abandons aggression rather than abandoning the helpless and embracing aggression. Such is the pathway to the Prince of Peace, the true light[233] and what Jesus always hoped for.

> May we choose to walk that pilgrimage together!
>
> May we profess our love before we proclaim our politics!
>
> And may we recall that "perfect love that casts out fear,"[234]
>
> the love which calls us to embrace light, eschew darkness, and care for one another!
>
> Amen.

---

233 John 1:9 He was the true light (*lux vera*), which enlightens everyone, the one who was coming into the world.

234 1 John 4:18.

LOVE

And he began to say unto them, "This day is this scripture fulfilled in your ears."[235]

When Jesus went out in public for the first time, he was dutifully accompanying his mother to a wedding reception where the wine ran out. Some clergy are not terribly enthusiastic about doing weddings. Much time is needed for proper preparation, counseling, paperwork, to say nothing of rehearsals that never start on time. Unless the funeral director is tardy, highly unusual, funerals do tend to start on time—despite the old saying about people who are predicted to be late for their own funeral. Not so. Despite all the lore around wedding ceremonies, including the silly questions, odd requests, and an occasional bridezilla—all that aside, I must categorically state that I love doing weddings.

A wedding is a joyful sacrament of new life, new hope, and new beginnings. The officiant can do a great deal to enhance this sacramental encounter, helping a couple fulfill their dreams. I performed my first wedding aboard a historic sailing ship. As a newly ordained transitional deacon, I was far less worried about getting seasick from the swaying ship than I was about doing the service right. I confessed right off to the couple, "This is my first wedding and I am not quite sure I know what I'm doing." They replied with a kindly

---

235 Luke 4:21 (KJV).

smile, "Oh, don't worry, Father, we know the routine pretty well. This is our third time around!" Well, that one sure broke any stray left-over ice in the harbor. The wedding went off without a hitch.

This beautiful collect,[236] though not actually part of the wedding service, would be suitable to ponder before exploring the perennially perplexing question, "What is love?"

> O God, you have taught us
> that without love whatever we do is worth nothing:
>
> Send your Holy Spirit and pour into our hearts
> your greatest gift, which is love,
> the true bond of peace and of all virtue,
> without which whoever lives
> is accounted dead before you.
>
> Grant this for the sake of your Son Jesus Christ,
> who lives and reigns with you and the Holy Spirit,
> one God, now and forever. *Amen.*

One of the nice things about preparing couples for marriage is having them pick out their own scriptural and non-scriptural readings. Invariably, an all-time favorite is First Corinthians 13, where Paul holds forth on the theme of *love*. In 1958, C.S. Lewis published a book entitled *The Four Loves*. In it, Lewis carefully discussed the various phases and faces of love by relating the English word *love* to its equivalents in Greek or Latin. Now English is a great language—don't get me wrong—but it often lets a single word express more than one nuance. This lexical piggybacking causes confusion. The English word *friend* is a good example. We refer to our *friends* at work, *friends* at church, or *friends* at the gym. Europeans are careful to use different words to distinguish

---

236 Collect for the Seventh Sunday after Epiphany, *BCP 1979*, p. 216.

casual acquaintances from genuine *personal friends*. American English, in particular, seldom makes such a distinction. When we talk about the word *love*, we are in a similar, perhaps even more acute dilemma. And regrettably, Hollywood has not helped matters at all. If anything, Tinsel Town has quite muddied the waters. C.S. Lewis, in his book *The Four Loves*,[237] tries to lay a suitable conceptual groundwork for understanding *love*. He distinguishes at least four aspects of human relationship which might fall under the umbrella of our one English word *love* devoting his last four chapters to each aspect:

- Chapter 3   Affection
- Chapter 4   Friendship
- Chapter 5   Eros
- Chapter 6   Charity

Affection is an introductory stage. We begin to like another person. We are drawn to making their acquaintance and enjoy being in their company. In a word, they speak our language. *Friendship* is the next stage or level of relationship where acquaintances move beyond mere affection for or liking one another. They become more than simply people whose first name we know. And this initial friendship, if it lasts, deepens and evolves to the point where the parties would go through thick and thin for one another. The highest stage of friendship is arrived at when both parties can count on one another's mutual loyalty. Somewhere during the growth and development of such a relationship, a European couple would agree to switch from using *formal* second-person address to using *familiar* address. In German, for example, they would switch from *Sie* to *du* or in French from *vous* to *tu*. Addressing the third stage, Lewis proceeds

---

[237]   C.S. Lewis, *The Four Loves* (New York: Harper Collins, 1960).

to describe *eros*, the Greek cognate with our word *erotic*. The strong friendship has now sufficiently evolved from purely *Platonic*[238] to one which includes deeper physical and emotional intimacy.

You might be wondering what could possibly come next? How much higher can one go in one's relationship with another? The answer is found in Lewis' sixth chapter which addresses the highest form of love, for which he uses the word *charity*. Once again, English begs for clarity. By using the word *charity*, Lewis is definitely not talking about donating goods or cash to a *charity*. In earlier usage, the English word *charity* expressed its Latin cognate *caritas*. And that Latin word *caritas*, as many Latin words do, has its Greek equivalent: *agape* (ἀγάπη).

What kind of love was Paul talking about in his letter to the Corinthian community? Writing in Greek, he was using ἀγάπη. His letter uses ἀγάπη throughout —never *eros* (*erotic love*), nor even *amicitia*, (friendship). And Paul's uniform use of ἀγάπη tells us something crucial to a proper understanding of Holy Matrimony. When couples choose 1 Corinthians 13, that text is not celebrating their transition from acquaintances to friends, and ultimately to lovers. No, none of that is what Paul is talking about. Paul is composing a hymn to the highest form of love, ἀγάπη love. No erstwhile copy editor decided the chapter sequence of *The Four Loves*. C.S. Lewis intentionally put the chapter on ἀγάπη after *eros*. The author is witnessing to a hierarchy of love, that selfless *agape* love, the *caritas* Jesus practiced, indeed the highest, most perfect, and most fulfilling aspect of human love. Couples who understand this when they pronounce their vows may during their life together achieve the highest expression of sacramental love.

Paul's letter to the Corinthians was in response to

---

[238] A Platonic relationship, named after the Greek philosopher Plato, is one considered devoid of romantic or sexual involvement.

questions from the community. They would occasionally seek his pastoral counsel. His *epistle*[239] was his vehicle to answer the community and provide pastoral clarification. Even back in Paul's time we can be sure there were questions about what *love* meant now for the followers of Jesus. Paul was in a unique position. He could look back to the birth of Christ as well forward to his passion, death, and resurrection. Paul was uniquely gifted to be able to tie it all together and encapsulate for these fledgling followers what *the love of Jesus* really meant. As a well-educated and now "completed" Jew, Paul was well-positioned to present Jesus the Messiah's wholly novel take on love: ἀγάπη, caritative love, the highest stage of love which asks absolutely nothing in return. And to explicate this radical redefinition was precisely Paul's goal in this letter. He wanted the Corinthian community to grasp and imitate the love Jesus himself showed, ἀγάπη, the love that embraces patience, perseverance, and politeness, as well as singleness of purpose.

> I am come that they might have life, and that they might have it more abundantly.[240]

His was a life of consistent love, constant *caritas*, enduring ἀγάπη. In placing ἀγάπη atop the pyramid, Jesus by no means was undervaluing human affection, friendship or romance. Throughout the developing stages of relationship, *more abundant life* must flow. All love must be tied together and blessed by ἀγάπη. Whether a relationship be casual or committed, ἀγάπη love is *the blessed tie that binds*.[241] If you

---

239 Derived from Greek ἐπιστολή or Latin *epistola* simply meaning letter.
240 John 10:10 (KJV).
241 "Blest be the tie that binds," a hymn written by John Fawcett (1739-1817), a dissenting Baptist clergyman in England. The entire first stanza reads: "Blest be the tie that binds / Our hearts in Christian love; / The fellowship of kindred minds / Is like to that above."

could imagine yourself posing the following question to Paul, how do you think he would respond?

> I know Jesus said he came to "bring us more abundant life." But how does one go about truly *living* in Christ? What does *more abundant life-in-Christ* look like?

I think he'd respond, "It looks like ἀγάπη." A tall but intriguing order, isn't it?

Motion

In 1701, the writer Daniel Defoe penned a poem he entitled *The True-born Englishman*. I remember learning it in college, whether in English or in theology I couldn't say. The poem begins with these words:

> Where're the Lord erects a house of prayer,
> The Devil always builds a chapel there;
> And 'twill be found, upon examination,
> The latter has the larger congregation.[242]

I couldn't say why those words stuck with me all these years, but to some extent, don't they reflect our present-day reality? From a physics class I recall learning Newton's so-called third law of motion.[243] If I push on anything, it pushes back on me. If I lean up against a wall, I don't just fall through it. The wall pushes back on me just as hard as I pushed on it, and so both of us stay in place. Throwing something puts more force behind it than just leaning up against an object. And so, it would push back with an equivalently greater force. The bigger the push, the bigger the push-back. That's why discharging a cannon or any gun makes it recoil. As the

---

[242] The original wording differs slightly: "Wherever God erects a house of prayer, the Devil always builds a chapel there; And 'twill be found, upon examination, the latter has the largest congregation."

[243] Newton's third law of motion states that for every action or force in nature there is an equal and opposite reaction. In other words, if object A exerts a force on object B, then object B also exerts an equal and opposite force back on object A.

cannon ball flies in one direction, the cannon itself moves in the opposite direction. How could this law of physics bear any relevance to Jesus' temptations in the wilderness?[244]

Jesus had spent a significantly long period of time, symbolized by the biblical number forty, on an intense retreat with his Father. He had hoped that this post-Baptismal retreat would help prepare him to launch his public ministry. It would likewise begin preparing him for his ultimate destiny, his passion and death on the cross. He needed to get ready for all this by intentionally seeking his Father and ultimate source of his divinity. The iambic pentameter of Defoe's poem, "Where're the Lord erects a house of prayer / the devil always builds a chapel there" comes back to haunt me whenever I ponder Jesus' temptations in the desert. Defoe's *house of prayer* would correspond to Jesus' desert lodging, a place of solace, calm, and peace. His prolonged fast would undoubtedly bring on massive hunger, but would simultaneously heighten his awareness of the Father's presence. Into this erstwhile serene environment none but Satan would dare intrude, the one who "always builds a chapel there." Lucifer's *chapels* are always built right over identical sites where the divine presence first held sway. You see, the *father of lies* enjoys superimposing his diabolical design right atop divine design. But Newton has stated that "every action has an equal and opposite reaction." Jesus' intense focus on contemplation draws the devil's equal and opposite reaction: temptation. Laser-focused on destroying the equilibrium in Jesus' soul, Satan seeks to sow doubt and confusion there. The devil is determined to prevent any sanctifying grace from coming to Jesus' aid. Lucifer would lessen if not totally obliterate the supreme sacrifice of the Son of man.

But let's not forget the corollary to Newton's third law,

---

244 Matthew 4:1-11; Mark 1:12-13; Luke 4:1-13.

that *the bigger the push, the bigger the push-back*. And didn't Jesus push back deftly in this encounter with evil! The devil may be the *Father of Lies*, but Jesus remains the *Son of Righteousness*. In the course of his three temptations, the devil mouths some half-truth or other, hoping to make a very hungry Jesus salivate. But the bigger the devil pushes falsehood the more Jesus pushes back with truth. Jesus calls Satan's faulty reasoning and disordered thinking for what it is, and thus prevails, one temptation at a time. Naturally, Jesus was starving after such a lengthy fast. Of course, being divine he had power to do anything he wanted, including turning stones into scones. But rather than buying into Satan's half-truth, Jesus was possessed of the whole truth, that we need more than bread to live on. One's hunger does not merit a miracle to suspend the laws of nature. Besides, it wasn't breakfast time yet, and furthermore, the last person in the world Jesus would want to break bread with was the devil.

Well, where would you and I visualize ourselves in this encounter? What might I really be hungry for? What would the worthiest object of my appetite be? Would I be humble enough to admit my spiritual hunger? Or might I just hunger for food, fun, and fulfillment? Have I ever taken time to prioritize my appetites? In the second temptation, the devil attempts to trick Jesus with a role reversal. He suggests Jesus worship *him* and promises that then *it all will be yours*. The devil thought that since Jesus was fasting, he had come upon him in a weakened, vulnerable, and debilitated state. He thought he could dupe Jesus into believing that Satan was divine and he was a mere human. Jesus pushes back here by quoting the first commandment: "Thou shalt worship the Lord thy God; and Him only shalt thou serve." That raises the question about whom or what *we* worship. Who is the *de facto* god of my life? Do I ever tend to get so confused that

I begin believing I am my own god? Do I think I can call the shots and arrange things to come my way? Well, as far as Jesus is concerned, we can call that strike two for the devil. But how would you and I handle those diabolical curve balls, especially when our appetites are raging?

Let me paraphrase the third temptation as the devil holds forth:

> "Do whatever you feel like. Risk whatever you like. No matter *what* you do, *presume* you'll be rescued. Don't forget Psalm 91 now, you know, the one that promises the fulltime protection of guardian angels, right? Have fun! Risk it all! Go for the gusto. Hey, you've got a blank check policy on any behavior and you only live once. So, just go and have fun! No matter *how* you behave, in the end you know your Father will fix it and you'll be just fine."

Jesus roundly contradicts that faulty theology by saying that I am not allowed to tempt God, to tempt fate, or to be careless with the gift of life I have been given. *Presumption* is but the flip side of *despair*: either we give up or we don't give a damn. Both are extremes. Both are *equal and opposite* sins. Jesus would not bite into *this* rotten apple either. We are called to moderation and caution with the gift of life. We are called to balance our dual roles as *wise serpents yet gentle doves*.[245] How do I approach life? Am I so deluded into thinking that I'll be rescued, no matter how recklessly I behave? Is the seatbelt law there to make me uncomfortable and restrict my freedom of movement? I'll just take a peek at that text message while barreling down the highway. Everything'll be fine. I won't get that distracted. And what about all that

---

245 The Latin is meaningful here: *prudentes sicut serpentes.*

research on smoking and vaping? That doesn't apply to me, does it? If I keep on drinking and drugging, there's no proof I'll become an addict, is there? Are my risks always *calculated* risks? Or will I get away with it because some other jerk will get caught not me? I'll be fine. These are questions worth pondering in any season of life not just during Lent. While the first three lines of Defoe's poem are true enough, allow me to rephrase his last line:

> Where're the Lord erects a house of prayer,
> The Devil always builds a chapel there;
>
> And 'twill be found, upon examination,
> The *former* has the larger congregation.

Yes, I'm praying that God's congregation will be the larger. I'm counting on major push-back lest the Devil get away with his typical trickery. I'm praying that you and I will be unafraid to do that "push back with equal and opposite force" and thereby counter diabolical deception with the unvarnished truth.

Naming

In Shakespeare's *Romeo and Juliet*, we hear Juliet pose a rhetorical question—and then propose her own answer:

> Juliet: What's in a name?
> That which we call a rose by any other name
> would smell as sweet.[246]

The issue of naming can go either way. It can be quite significant or rather insignificant. Sometimes babies' names are picked at random, out of a hat, seemingly out of nowhere; occasionally prospective parents may use a name book; sometimes names are derivatives of some family name. The whole process is by no means any straight-line, traditional enterprise.

Years ago, within the milieu of the Roman Catholic world, children's names were chosen by the saint's name closest to their birthday on the liturgical calendar. My mother, for example, who was born on January 19th was baptized "Agnes" because the nearest female feastday was St. Agnes of Rome on January 21st. I was baptized "John Edward" simply because that was my Dad's name. Nowadays, to older ears, we hear some of the wildest names with an even wilder orthography, including accents and/or other diacritic marks. The emphasis is on being unique rather than relating to saints or relatives. Good luck trying to spell (never mind pronounce) some of those novel names correctly!

---

246 *Romeo and Juliet* (ll, ii, 1-2).

In other cases, names actually do have both rhyme and reason, as they seek to express some characteristic related to the person. In the ancient classical world, there was a notion that *nomen est omen*,[247] your name is your omen, implying that how one is named would describe their destiny. In other words, the selection of a certain name would hopefully chart one's future. We baptized our second granddaughter "Kailani Grace." In Hawaiian, Kailani can be interpreted as "the heavenly waters," or "the sea and sky," or "the water come down from heaven." And as Christians, we know what we mean by *grace*.

In the liturgy of a High Mass, after the altar has been censed, the celebrant generally performs the *Rite of Sprinkling* known as the *Asperges*. If you ever have attended such a liturgy, you probably sensed some of these tiny droplets of Holy Water coming your way. Newcomers, often caught unawares, sometimes conclude the roof must be leaking. Those droplets are quite intentionally sprinkled. The Rite of Sprinkling over the assembly signifies our reclaiming the waters of our own baptism, however long ago that might have been. Water purifies. Water blesses. Water renews. Water is holy. A wonderful, haunting Advent hymn known as the *Rorate caeli* implores God to open the clouds of heavens and "rain down upon us the Just One," meaning to rain down upon us Christ the Savior, the Babe of Bethlehem, the long-expected Jesus for whom one waits during Adventide.

Whenever I perform the *Asperges* during a Baptismal Mass, I beg God to rain down upon every baptismal candidate nothing less than the Savior's unmitigated grace. And I likewise invite each congregant to pray that their own baptismal name may in a certain spiritual sense suggest their holy destiny. Someday, Jesus the Good Shepherd will be

---

247 Greek όνομα ορίζοντας.

calling out to us by that name and we need to be attentive to His voice.

Every fourth Sunday after Easter is celebrated as *Good Shepherd* Sunday. Naming Jesus as the *Good Shepherd*, is extremely important since it identifies his unique role in salvation history. The opening collect on Good Shepherd Sunday asks God to "grant that when we hear his voice, we may know him who calls us each by name."[248]

And in the Gospel Jesus himself prays that "they will listen to my voice."[249]

Jesus calls us each of us by name in the sincere hope that we will be well attuned to his voice, and will clearly recognize the Good Shepherd calling us by our baptismal name.

Every Fourth Sunday of Easter, Good Shepherd Sunday, the image of a certain phonograph record label always pops back into my head—that's right, not a compact disc label but a phonograph record. The red RCA Victor label had the picture of an old-fashioned, hand-cranked "Victrola" with a little white dog listening intently to its sound. The caption read, "His Master's Voice." The dog looking up attentively and devotedly at the machine recognized the voice emanating from it. Quaint perhaps, but still very effective for me to recall Jesus' words:

> My sheep hear my voice; I know them,
> and they follow me.[250]

And as he had just said a bit earlier:

> I am the good shepherd. I know mine and
> mine know me.[251]

---

248 Collect for the Fourth Sunday after Easter.
249 John 10:16.
250 John 10:27.
251 John 10:14.

The earliest Christians came under heavy persecution. Apostles were challenged to stand up or stand down as to Jesus' identity. The authorities were taking names and kicking butt, as the expression goes, but their spokesperson was undeterred. Having advanced this far in his spiritual development, Peter had now become incredibly bold and totally forthright about whom he was naming and with whom he was identifying:

> When [the authorities] had made the prisoners stand in their midst, they inquired, "By what power or by what name did you do this?" Then Peter, filled with the Holy Spirit, said to them, "Rulers of the people and elders, if we are questioned today because of a good deed done to someone who was sick and are asked how this man has been healed, let it be known to all of you, and to all the people of Israel, that this man is standing before you in good health by the name of Jesus Christ of Nazareth, whom you crucified, whom God raised from the dead.[252]

And that inspiring passage from the fourth chapter of Acts doesn't end there either. It goes on to attest mightily to the healing power of Jesus. I love this scripture, part of our liturgy of the healing anointing. It pulls no punches about either the name or the identity of the healer:

> There is salvation in no one else, for there is no other name under heaven given among mortals by which we are to be be saved.[253]

---

[252] Acts 4:7-10.
[253] Acts 4:12.

Names *are* powerful. Names *can* convey distinct meaning. If we listen attentively to the Good Shepherd, if we hear our Master's voice; if we decide to cooperate with God's grace; our baptismal *nomen* can truly become our *omen* and chart the destiny of our Resurrection Life.

NATURE

Almighty God,
You have given your only-begotten Son
To take our nature upon Him,
And to be born this day of a pure virgin:
Grant that we, who have been born again...
May be daily renewed by your Holy Spirit.

This Christmas Collect raises important yet challenging theological questions. Who is taking whose nature upon whom? And precisely what baby is getting born on Christmas? This collect is saying that by his birth, Jesus is making a conscious choice to take upon Himself our *human nature*. But how does that work? Is somehow a human nature superimposed onto a preexisting divine nature? The mechanics of it all seem challenging. Let's have a look.

If the Holy Trinity (God in three persons) is *eternal*, that would mean that God had always existed in three distinct persons, right? For lack of more accurate vocabulary, these three have traditionally been referred to as *Father, Son*, and *Holy Spirit*. A laboratory scientist might just as well have coded them Persons A, B & C, or Persons 1, 2 & 3. St. John calls Person 2 the *Word*.[254] Since God is a spirit,[255] how the three persons are titled is arbitrary.

---

254 John 1:1 "In the beginning was the Word, and the Word was with God, and the Word was God." "*In principio erat verbum, et verbum erat apud Deum et Deus erat verbum.*"

255 John 4:24.

So, just for the purpose of discussion, let's refer to the Second Person of the Trinity as *Divine Person B*. This avoids using either *Son* or *Word*. If God is *eternal*, then *Divine Person B* is also eternal and must have always existed as well. Somewhere in time, we know not exactly when, God created human beings[256] thereby launching the human family. Almost from day one, human beings began to behave badly by disobeying rules. Such bad behavior[257] moved God to make a course correction. The Creator had to come up with some divine strategy to restore order. The plan God came up with was to send *Divine Person B* to the rescue. But the eternal *Word* was not destined to come in pure spirit form. *Divine Person B* would have to be born as a regular human being, just like you or me. He would have a name, Jesus, and in one sense be quite ordinary, but in another, quite extraordinary. And this is where Christmas came from in the first place: God's plan to rescue a fallen humanity.

Since creation, human nature as depicted in the metaphorical Garden of Eden unfortunately started off on the wrong foot. This all happened long before Jesus Christ came on the scene. But by being born among us, God gave humankind a second chance to obey and at least try to get it right. The collect affirms that *Divine Person* B voluntarily took on our human nature. At Jesus' birth, his *flawless divine nature* was forever fused with our *flawed human nature*. Another word for *Incarnation* is *en-fleshment*. Preexisting *Divine Person* B would now receive a second nature, namely *human* nature. *Divine Person* B intentionally chose to share the very same humanity of our progenitors, created many millennia before. The fusion of our humanity with his divinity was irrevocable. The Incarnation could not be reversed and there was no way back, either for God or for humankind. Once Jesus got born,

---
256 Genesis 1:26-27.
257 Genesis 3:1-7, traditionally referred to as "original sin."

we got born again as well. That's precisely what is meant by our *second birth* or by the expression "born again" or "born from above."

> Grant that we, who have been born again...
> May be daily renewed by your Holy Spirit.

In praying that collect we not only *admit* to our second birth, we *claim* it. And that's why Christmas is so absolutely foundational to our self-identity. We must come to grips with how the Christ-event has *divinized* us. The beautiful mystical theology of that realization notwithstanding, the Christ-event prompts us to further considerations. Isaiah's prophecy is not just historical, but applies well beyond those who lived when Jesus did:

> The people who walked in darkness have seen a great light; those who lived in a land of deep darkness, on them light has shined.[258]

What is the land of deep darkness I'm currently mired in? Just one verse before, it says "there will be no more gloom for those who were in anguish."[259] That's awfully good news I desperately need to hear because I've already experienced more than enough gloom and doom, death and darkness. Isaiah is writing me a blank check to cover it all. But am I aware that, thanks to the Christ-event, I now have every opportunity to be born anew? How do I feel about that? Given the Incarnation, given God's en-fleshment, how do I feel about God being all mixed up in my own DNA? From the theology of the Christ-event, it would appear that God and we humans are in it for the long haul. There's no way back to how things used to be before that very first Christmas. And thank God for that!

---

258 Isaiah 9:2.
259 Isaiah 9:1.

Obedience

Whenever an angel appears to a saint, that saint usually gets up, goes, and does whatever the angel said to. I don't know about you, but I doubt I'd ever be able to move quite that fast, especially if the angel chose to show up in the morning. But at least one person we know from scripture did seem to waste no time and that person would be Philip.[260] Philip's saga is one of the holiest and funniest encounters in the entire New Testament. Philip did promptly get up out of bed that morning and went exactly where the angel told him, without benefit of GPS. And the angel handed him no roadmap. He provided no directions at all. Philip was simply told to go stand on the corner of some vague intersection in the desert and wait.

But despite all that, Philip obeyed and went, somehow getting to the right place at the right time. There must be something about listening to the Master's voice, ever ready to hear from the Good Shepherd. Someone once quipped that in the spiritual life you don't have to know where you are going; you just have to know whom you're following. Philip fit that mindset when he acknowledged the angel as an authentic messenger of the Lord. More proof would have been superfluous. Well, here is where obedience intersects with hilarity in how he had to carry his mission out.

Clippety-clop, along comes a rather sumptuously-appointed, six-horsepower chariot, the private limo for a

---

260 Acts 8:26-40.

certain Ethiopian VIP, namely the Treasury Secretary. He had been attending an Annual Convention where books must have been available for purchase. So, to while away the time traveling back home, he picked himself up a nice leather-bound copy of the Hebrew Bible and started off trying to read the prophet Isaiah. To help time pass even more quickly on this long, boring trip across the desert in the chariot, he was reading the text out loud. Here is this fellow, curious yet clueless, rattling off words from Isaiah without the faintest idea what they meant. If Philip himself had had to pass time on such a journey, he would have picked anything but Isaiah to read. But somehow, the words of Isaiah held the interest of this celebrity traveler for quite some time. That scene is funny enough in itself, but gets even funnier. When Philip sees the chariot racing toward the intersection where he was standing, he hears the traveler mumbling words from Isaiah. He resists laughing and starts running alongside the fast-moving chariot. An incredible scene.

As an ice-breaker, Philip asks this total stranger whether he gets what he's reading. Maybe from the fellow's pronunciation Philip could tell the text wasn't making any sense to him. Well, the Ethiopian official invites Philip to hop into the chariot and sit alongside him. There is no mention that he even stopped the chariot to pick him up. Philip just hops aboard while it's still moving and parks himself next to this clueless yet curious reader:

> Philip ran up and heard him reading Isaiah the prophet and said, "Do you understand what you are reading?" He replied, "How can I, unless someone explains it to me?" So, he invited Philip to get in and sit with him.[261]

He *invited* Philip to get in and sit with him. He desires to

---

[261] Acts 8:30-31.

make sense out of what he is reading rather than just rattling off a bunch of words. Somehow, God has caught this Gentile's attention. And only now does Philip intuit why the angel told him to get up and go stand in the middle of nowhere. Only now does he see how his obedience has paid off. The angel's voice channeled the voice of the Good Shepherd when he said:

> And other sheep I have, which are not of this fold: them also I must bring, and they shall hear my voice; and there shall be one fold, and one shepherd.[262]

This was to be Philip's mission, sent to evangelize one of those *other sheep*, to bring Good News to a heart and soul seeking God's love. Philip explained the passage so effectively that his fellow traveler asked why he couldn't be baptized right then and there. Suddenly a pool of water pops up along their route. But they're crossing the desert where pools of water are virtually nonexistent. But in this incredible tale of faithful obedience, we see again that God provides. Water appears and this traveler asks why he can't be baptized.

How had Philip been so well prepared to follow the angel's direction? How many times have you and I just turned over and gone back to sleep after a dream, without giving any possible meaning a second thought? How was Philip able so promptly to respond to God's messenger? How had he become so attuned that he was able to listen deeply?[263] By the time of his dream, Philip had already become so thoroughly grafted onto Christ's vine[264] that he would even go to an unknown spot to share the Gospel with a total stranger.

---

[262] John 10:16 (KJV).
[263] The root meaning of obedience is from Latin *ob-audire*, to listen deeply.
[264] John 15:5. "I am the vine, you are the branches. Those who abide in me and I in them bear much fruit, because apart from me you can do nothing." (NRSV).

You or I probably won't be asked to run after some chariot in the desert nor to hop aboard while it's still moving. We'll probably be called to share the Good News some other far less dramatic way.

Jesus *wants* mutual abiding,[265] we in him and he in us. He *wants* to settle down and make his home within us! He *wants* to fashion us into living tabernacles! He invites us to that intimacy. "If today you hear his voice, harden not your hearts."[266]

---

265 John 15:3. "Abide in me as I abide in you. Just as the branch cannot bear fruit by itself unless it abides in the vine, neither can you, unless you abide in me." (NRSV).

266 Psalm 95:8.

Refreshment

Some parts of the country tend to get far too little rain. That can be a real problem. But there are wider implications of *drought*, whether they be of a physical or spiritual nature. You can cut down somewhat and thereby neither overuse nor waste water, but what do you do if you become spiritually arid and almost completely dry up? In that case, only the holy water of heaven can satisfy our spiritual thirst. Especially if we thirst for justice and peace, we are in need of the true Messiah to arrive and deliver Living Water. One day Jesus showed up "unexpectedly" at Jacob's well, where an amazing interaction took place. On a pilgrimage to the Holy Land, we got to drink from that actual, very deep well. The water was pure, cool, and refreshing. Truly, this was holy water:

> The woman [at the well] said to him, "Sir, you have no bucket, and the well is deep. Where do you get that living water?"[267]

The *Rite of Sprinkling* at Mass is often accompanied by chanting the *Rorate caeli*,[268] an ancient plainsong begging God to rain down the Messiah upon us. Lest we miss the point, Isaiah takes pains to stress the necessary relationship between watering and growth:

---

267 John 4:11.
268 *Rorate caeli desuper et nubes pluant justum.* Drop down dew, ye heavens, from above, and let the clouds rain down the Just One.

> The wilderness and the dry land shall be glad, the desert shall rejoice and blossom; like the crocus it shall blossom abundantly, and rejoice with joy and singing.[269]
>
> For waters shall break forth in the wilderness, and streams in the desert; the burning sand shall become a pool, and the thirsty ground springs of water.[270]
>
> Everlasting joy shall be upon their heads; they shall obtain joy and gladness, and sorrow and sighing shall flee away.[271]

These words not only recall our need for spiritual irrigation, but also promise rejoicing, gladness, and abundance. The Messiah will finally arrive to relieve our parched, desiccated humanity and move us forward along our spiritual pilgrimage. Isaiah promises not only rain but refreshment and rejoicing. There is one Sunday of the church year with some special titles: *Rose* Sunday, *Refreshment* Sunday, or *Rejoice* Sunday. Half-way through the waiting season of Advent we are encouraged to take a break from our introspection to anticipate the future. Whom are we waiting for? For the *Just One* to be rained down upon us from above. Advent invites us to reflection not remorse, to thoughtfulness not anxiety. *Rose Sunday* derives its designation from the custom of using rose-colored vestments and paraments to remind us to be joyful because we are awaiting our Messiah. The holiness of Advent waiting also finds beautiful expression in an epistle:

> Be patient, therefore, beloved, until the coming of the Lord. The farmer waits for

---

[269] Isaiah 35:1-2.
[270] Isaiah 35:6-7.
[271] Isaiah 35:10.

the precious crop from the earth, being
patient with it until it receives the early
and the late rains. You also must be
patient. Strengthen your hearts, for the
coming of the Lord is near. As an example
of suffering and patience, beloved, take
the prophets who spoke in the name of
the Lord.[272]

Waiting for the ultimate refreshment that only the Messiah can bring implies *patient, purposeful, and joyful* waiting. One gospel writer offers a helpful proverb:

By exercising your patience, you will
possess your souls.[273]

The December crescendo builds toward the climax of Christmas Day. But it has very little to do with the debut of Jesus Christ. It bears little relationship to a Savior preparing to enter the unfolding drama of our salvation history. December itself can offer only minimal refreshment. Those "twenty-four shopping days left till Christmas" are much more about an annual commercial hustle than quiet, reflective preparation. Refreshment Sunday, coming right in mid-Advent, however, is all about genuine refreshment.

May the holy water of heaven fall softly upon you.
May Living Waters drench your soul.
May you anticipate the refreshment
of the Christ Child.
And may you receive not just rain,
but also refreshment.
As Mary, may you ponder these things
in your heart.

---

272 James 5:7-8, 10.
273 Luke 21:19. *In patientia vestra possidebitis animas vestras.*

Repentance

If you compare Mark's gospel with the other two synoptics, you will discover how silent he is about so many details of the life of Christ. Matthew and Luke flesh out the story in much fuller detail. In six short verses, Mark very tersely summarizes Jesus' baptism in the Jordan, his forty desert days (without going into his temptations), and the arrest of his first cousin, John the Baptist, as Jesus picks up his prophetic ministry. Mark skips the little detail about John's destiny as the forerunner of Jesus. We find this in first chapter of Luke, where Zechariah prophesies about the destiny of his newborn son:

> And you, child, will be called the prophet
> of the Most High; for you will go before
> the Lord to prepare his ways, to give
> knowledge of salvation to his people by
> the forgiveness of their sins.[274]

Mark leaves out many important details, providing but a bare outline. His opening verses are, however, surprisingly complete and quite significant:

> In those days Jesus came from Nazareth
> of Galilee and was baptized by John in
> the Jordan. And just as he was coming
> up out of the water, he saw the heavens

---

[274] Luke 1:76-77.

torn apart and the Spirit descending like a dove on him. And a voice came from heaven, "You are my Son, the Beloved; with you I am well pleased."[275]

Mark's account of Jesus' baptism is particularly noteworthy since the words spoken by God exactly parallel those spoken at Jesus' transfiguration:

Then a cloud overshadowed them, and from the cloud there came a voice, "This is my Son, the Beloved; listen to him!" Suddenly when they looked around, they saw no one with them anymore, but only Jesus.[276]

Remember that at the moment of transfiguration both Moses and Elijah disappear once the cloud has lifted. From now on, *only Jesus* was to be speaking, *only Jesus* was the one to be listened to. That occurrence corrected Peter's misguided notion about erecting *three* shrines. Only one, the new one, the very temple of the New Jerusalem, was to be built. A new world order would be called into being and established, based solely on Jesus' threefold ministry of prophet, priest, and king.

The exterior, external, and superficial were now superseded by the interior, internal, and profound. Jesus would devote most of his public ministry to modeling that paradigm shift. The Ash Wednesday liturgy offers worshipers the option of having sacred ashes traced on their foreheads in the sign of the cross. There are two possible formulas for imposing ashes, either *Remember that you are dust, and to dust you shall return*, or *Repent, and believe in the good*

---

[275] Mark 1:9-11.
[276] Mark 9:7-8.

news. Deriving from Genesis, the first formula is the more traditional and familiar:

> By the sweat of your face you shall eat bread, until you return to the ground, for out of it you were taken; for you are dust, and to dust you shall return.[277]

This older formula, more penitential, admonishes the worshiper. This familiar scene from the Garden of Eden shows the Creator disciplining his disobedient creature Adam by reminding him of his origins. This text likewise reminds us where we came from and where we are headed, returning to the elements whence we came, cremation being the most literal fulfillment of these words. When I add up how much I will have spent on clothing and cosmetics during my earthly sojourn, my inescapable return to ashes certainly gives me pause. How might that money have been better invested? But is this the message I need to hear on the first day of Lent? Maybe yes, maybe no. While without doubt a sobering reminder, I question whether it encourages me to develop my spiritual life in a more positive direction.

In the Middle Ages, monks passing one another along the cloister walk would not exchange pleasantries nor even raise their downcast glance from the path. Without so much as looking at one another they would exchange two words: *memento mori*, remember death. Not a very cheery greeting for sure. But the medieval mind emphasized eschatology over cheerfulness. Medieval monastics focused on the so-called four last things: *death, judgment, heaven, and hell* rather than engage in superficial chit-chat. Would we in our own day adopt their mantra as well? I think not, because for one thing, it does not square with our last eight centuries of theological

---

[277] Genesis 3:19.

development nor does it align with how we understand *repentance*.

The alternative formula for the imposition of ashes differs markedly from the traditional one. It's also scriptural but shorter and drawn from the New rather than from the Old Testament:

> Repent and believe in the good news.[278]

The alternative formula exhibits a decidedly different theological emphasis. This scripture does not peer into the rearview mirror and remind us of our humble origins from worthless dust. Rather, this scripture makes us face ourselves squarely wherever we are right now. The invitation to *repent*, as properly understood today, means to "turn our life around." That's understanding *repentance* as a serious reorientation of lifestyle, one which strives for the goal of a radical 180 degree turn. The *pen* part of the word *repentance* does not imply doing *penance* or going to a *penitentiary*, nor does it connote *punishment*. These words look and sound alike and therefore often get mixed up. And if *repentance* is misheard and thus misconstrued, the encouraging thrust of Jesus' words goes unheard. Jesus encourages us to reset our life's compass. By doing just that, we are more and more drawn to embrace the good news he brought us. The new world order of Jesus exchanges quantity for quality, head for heart, and hate for love. Listen to the Father's words in Matthew's account of the Transfiguration:

> This is my beloved Son, in whom I am well pleased; hear ye him.[279]

---

278 Mark 1:15.
279 Matthew 17:5 (KJV).

What would God's Son say if *he* were the one administering the ashes? I doubt he'd utter with downcast glance the words *memento mori* as he approached us. I doubt he'd remind us that we had our origins in dust and that's where we're headed back when it's all over. I'd rather imagine Jesus looking me straight in the eye, smiling and connecting with me very much in the moment. Of course, he'd know exactly where I happened to be along my journey. But rather than chastise me sternly for my transgressions, he'd smile and encourage me during Lent to continue working at realigning my life with his. He'd want me to face him, to look him squarely in the eye, rather than looking downward or wasting my time gazing upon lesser gods. Jesus would encourage me to live the journey, rather than focusing on its beginning or its end. He would ask me to remember that

> The time is fulfilled, and the kingdom of God has come near. [It's now an auspicious time to] repent and believe in the good news.[280]

---

280 Mark 1:15.

ROSES

An old German proverb reminds us of the obvious fact that roses have thorns.[281] I'm definitely no gardener, no green thumb, but by now I would guess science has probably canceled out the truth of that old adage. There must be some genetically modified roses that have no thorns, just like seedless grapes. I doubt whether grapes with seeds even still exist. Surely have not seen any at the supermarket lately. But in any case, the point of the old German proverb is that beauty seldom exists in its apparently flawless form. Roses, which have merited universal favor for their beauty, as well as their ability to curry female favor, still pose a nasty threat: thorns! Something exists to interfere with the ecstasy of beholding the rose: the thorn that will wound you if you don't handle it carefully.

On two Sundays of the year, most liturgical churches celebrate *Rose Sunday*.[282] The colorful rose-pink vestments and hangings soften the somber violet-purple generally worn in either season. The theological point of celebrating a Rose Sunday in Advent or in Lent is to create a liturgical half-time affording a pause that refreshes. In Lent, *Laetare* Sunday offers respite before engaging the rigors of Holy Week. In Advent, *Gaudete Sunday*[283] reminds us not to surrender to a

---
[281] *Keine Rose ohne Dornen.*
[282] The third Sunday in Advent and the fourth in Lent.
[283] *Laetare* and *Gaudete* are Latin synonyms for "rejoice." They were the opening words of the older liturgies of each respective season.

frenetic, consumer-driven December. It is time for a rose-colored refocus on what Advent is about, not about shopping but about waiting for Jesus to be born.

Where is our spiritual bouquet of roses in all this? What are we supposed to get out of this color change? Rose is a decidedly lighter color than purple, one which mutes the darker, more somber color purple. The overall scriptural theme for both Sundays is *light*.

> For once you were darkness, but now in the Lord you are light. Live as children of light— for the fruit of the light is found in all that is good and right and true.[284]

We are urged to become children of *light*, and reminded that *light* produces every kind of goodness, justice, and truth.

> Everything exposed by the light becomes visible, for everything that becomes visible is light.[285]

We are advised to take no part in deeds done in *darkness* which bear no fruit. That phrase was an eye-opener for me. I'm neither scientist nor gardener, but it would stand to reason that no one would leave most plants in a dark room and expect them to grow. Some plants do better in partial shade, but I've never heard of plants that thrive in total darkness. The term *photosynthesis* refers to what goes on in plants exposed to *sunlight*. Most plants need sunlight or at least some type of light in order to thrive.

When I was a university professor, I remember when the state law changed to affect our faculty meetings. The so-called "sunshine law" meant that proceedings had to be open

---

284 Ephesians 5:8-9.
285 Ephesians 5:13-14.

to the public, except when in executive session. A *sunshine law*. Both theologically and botanically appropriate! No more unhealthy, smoke-filled back rooms, no more dark secrets, no more fertile breeding ground for non-transparency. And not only plants need photosynthesis. We do, too, *spiritual photosynthesis*. Paul expresses this in a most striking way:

> The night is far gone, the day is near. Let
> us then lay aside the works of darkness
> and put on the armor of light.[286]

The imagery is abundantly clear. We are urged to cast off and discard our tattered, filthy, disgusting rags, and redress ourselves in much more beautiful and brighter clothes. We are to abandon darkness, secrecy, and stealth in favor of light, transparency, and visibility. Bach's famous hymn tune *Wachet auf* emerges from my musical memory whenever I hear these words:

> Everything that becomes visible is light.
> Therefore, it says, "Sleeper, awake! Rise
> from the dead, and Christ will give you
> light."[287]

Light is where our souls naturally seek to dwell rather than in darkness. No sane soul would naturally prefer to "walk through the valley of the shadow of spiritual death" rather than to "dwell in the house of the Lord forever."[288] When Jesus prepares to heal the man blind from birth, he exclaims:

> We must work the works of him who sent

---

286 Romans 13:12. *Nox praecessit; dies autem appropinquavit. Abiciamus ergo opera tenebrarum, et induamur arma lucis.*
287 Ephesians 5:14.
288 Psalm 23.

me while it is day; night is coming when no one can work. As long as I am in the world, I am the light of the world."[289]

Light versus darkness. Jesus knows that darkness and death are soon coming his way. The light of Christ, the *lumen Christi*, must continue to illuminate and heal as long as the Christ Light is still present. Jesus summarizes this event while admonishing his onlookers by saying:

> "I came into this world for judgement so that those who do not see may see, and those who do see may become blind." Some of the Pharisees near him heard this and said to him, "Surely we are not blind, are we?" Jesus said to them, "If you were blind, you would not have sin. But now that you say, 'We see,' your sin remains."[290]

Whether I say *gaudete* or *laetare* at mid-season, I need to rejoice that there is light at the end of my tunnel. Regardless which tunnel I might currently inhabit, our Lord wants me at least to look for that rosy glow at tunnel's end.

---

[289] John 9:4-5.
[290] John 9:39-41.

SACRAMENTS

Jesus, starting with his birth at Bethlehem, his baptism at the River Jordan and later as a young adult, continues to manifest himself to us sacramentally. How do we understand a *Sacrament* in the upper-case sense? And what do we mean by *sacramentals*, or sacramental moments in a lower-case sense? What are some special life events that can occur at any time or place? But first, before we delve into such heady questions, let me share a little wedding story, that special life event where two persons have been said to "commit matrimony." Recently, while paging through a book, out fell a very old yellowed news clipping from an advice column. Apparently, some Roman Catholic bishop had written in complaining how much he disliked doing weddings. This generated a firestorm of responses, many from clergy who agreed with the bishop. They shared their own less-than-enthusiastic attitudes towards doing weddings. This banter reminded me of the snarky, tongue-in-cheek response I made to one woman who asked if she could have her new grandchild *done* at my parish. I asked the lady *how* she wanted the baby done: "medium-rare or well?" As I recall, she hung up on me.

Many of the curious stories from advice columnists about weddings probably actually happened. Some priest in Buffalo NY wrote in that the mother of a bride had phoned him to ask what material the church was made of. I was already formulating the kind of wisecrack I would have come back with. Well, this rather non-wisecracking Buffalo priest simply said *stone*. "Oh," replied the distraught mother-of-the-bride, "that simply won't do. We're looking for a wooden church." Can you imagine? Another bride called in to inquire if her dog could walk her down the aisle. "Are you blind?" the priest asked. She replied, "Oh no, not at all. It's just that Buster is a member of the family and he would be so hurt if he weren't included." Well, maybe that's because the word GOD is DOG spelled backwards? Truth *can be* stranger than fiction. In one sense, these stories make us laugh. But in another, they bespeak a woeful misunderstanding of the Sacraments of the Church, of which Holy Matrimony is one. Parish churches are not wedding chapels, and the parish priest is no concierge. Parishes exist to teach and to administer the sacraments, including *Holy Baptism* and *Holy Matrimony*, *holy* being the operative word. These are sacramental and not secular events. The Sacraments of Holy Baptism and Holy Matrimony were not something the Church dreamed up. Both have Gospel sources: (1) Jesus' own baptism;[291] and (2) his first miracle at a wedding.[292] Those attending weddings are reminded about this:

> Dearly beloved: We have come together in the presence of God to witness and bless the joining together of this couple in Holy Matrimony. The bond and covenant of marriage was established by God in creation, and our Lord Jesus Christ adorned this manner of life by his presence and first miracle at a wedding in Cana of Galilee.[293]

At the time this wedding took place, Jesus was probably

---

[291] Reported in all three synoptics: Matthew 3:13-17; Mark 1:9-11; Luke 3:21-22.
[292] John 2:11 "Jesus did this, the first of his signs, in Cana of Galilee, and revealed his glory; and his disciples believed in him."
[293] *BCP 1979*, p. 423.

about thirty. Just shortly before this event, he had been baptized. And his first disciples, formerly his cousin John's, were now following him. This "gang of four," including Jesus, now hung out practically all the time. These followers were attracted both by his message and his personhood. *Disciple* means *student* and *rabbi* means teacher. With Jesus as their rabbi, these few would soon grow to twelve. Jesus' mother Mary had been invited to this wedding. Her twenty-something son and his three BFFs came along as well. No engraved invitations were delivered in those days. People heard about the event and showed up. That presents no problem at all, at least until the wine runs out! And, of course, we know that it did. That's where the sacramental segment of our story begins. Mary tells Jesus about the wine problem. Jesus' reply is curt and concise, as are Mary's words to the wait staff:

> Jesus' mother told him, "They have no wine." Jesus replied, "Mother, what does that have to do with me? My hour has not yet come." She instructed those waiting on tables, "Do whatever he tells you."[294]

Those exchanges hardly qualify as a conversation. But they shed light on the steadily evolving personhood of Jesus. He pushes back when Mary subtly suggests that he could fix things. She knew who her son was: Jesus, *Yeshua ha-Mashiach*, Messiah and Deity. She just drops him a not-so-subtle hint. She doesn't argue with him nor as his mother order him to obey. She just has a keen sense that he'll hear her request, follow through, and fix the wine problem.

The wedding at Cana could inspire a beautiful triptych, *The Threefold Icon of Obedience*. Mary *obeys* the Holy Spirit

---

[294] John 2:4-5.

by asking her son a favor, albeit a premature request; Jesus *obeys* Mary and turns ordinary water into extraordinary wine; and the servants *obey* Mary by taking direction from her son. This triptych would reveal the virtue of obedience in its root meaning, the practice of *deep listening*. Jesus heard Mary's gentle request. She didn't even have to ask him directly. Mary knows about the divinity of her son. Jesus reminds her it wasn't quite yet time for his public ministry to begin. Mary listens to his response without objection. But by directing the servers to listen to Jesus' instructions, she is silently reassuring her son that his moment *was* already here. "Don't be afraid. Just go ahead and begin." That was the *cor ad cor loquitur*[295] moment of unspoken dialog between Mary and Jesus, two human beings who shared the same flesh and spirit. Graciously yielding to his Blessed Mother, Jesus performed this first miracle, launching his ministry earlier than even he had anticipated. This scene makes me think of a parent standing beside a child who is learning to walk or to ride a bike for the first time. For Jesus, this was a virtual *training wheels* moment. Much more involved and less pedestrian miracles would follow, but Jesus would always recall this first one, his debut sacramental moment.

What is my own personal sacramental story? Which Sacraments or sacramental events have shaped the course of my life? How might I enter more deeply into the sacramental nature of faith, hope, love, belonging, and obedience?

---

295 A year before his death in 1879, John Henry Newman, created Cardinal by Pope Leo XIII, chose as his motto *Cor ad cor loquitur*, heart speaks to heart.

SHINING

Grant that your people,
illumined by your Word and Sacraments,
may shine with the radiance of Christ's glory.[296]

The language of some prayers, even in contemporary wording, can come across a bit too poetical, idealistic or hifalutin. How often nowadays does anyone ever get *illumined*? But language aside, we might wonder *how we do shine*, if ever? We hear the word *shine* more frequently than the word *illumine*. *Shine* is one of those one syllable, Anglo-Saxon words. *Illumine*, on the other hand, is one of those fancier poly-syllabic Latin-based words. So, for now, let's stay with *shine* and explore how we *can* shine, or if we don't, how we might. Clues are to be found all over the Bible. Let's begin with a verse from Isaiah:

> Listen to me, O coastlands, pay attention, you peoples from far away! The LORD called me before I was born, while I was in my mother's womb, he named me.[297]

The Greeks are said somehow always to have a word for it. One of their pithiest sayings was this two-word sentence: *gnothi s'auton*, know yourself. If we are ever to shine in life,

---

296 *BCP 1979*, p. 215 from the Collect for the Second Sunday after Epiphany.
297 Isaiah 49:1.

in the sense of operating at our highest human potential, we first need to know who we are, our *true self*, as Thomas Merton, Richard Rohr, and many others have taught. Without adequate self-knowledge, rather than *shining* we are more apt to bungle our way through life, seldom able to relate with others more than superficially.

To *shine*, to be the best version of ourselves, we first need to deal with our true self, minus any masks or facades we wear. We often try to hide our true identity from others as well as from ourselves. Isaiah reveals that from the moment God dreamt us up, God already had various ideal plans in mind for us. Knowing our true self is the gateway to discovering those possibilities. I can never live "a purpose-driven life"[298] unless I know who I really am. If driven by *my* plans rather than God's, my life will not shine as brightly as it might have. People don't discover how uniquely God designed them mainly for two main reasons: first, they skip doing the necessary math for self-discovery; and second, people engage in negative self-talk. They tell themselves how rotten, useless, and bad they are. And we don't usually dream up a negative self-image all by ourselves. It often echoes criticisms projected upon us by others, especially by parents, teachers, and employers. God, designer of all, is not glorified when we ourselves or anyone else says bad things about his design:

> For you make me jubilant, Lord, by your deeds;
> at the works of your hands I shout for joy.
>
> How great are your works, Lord!
> How profound your designs![299]

Regardless what criticism might come at us from outside,

---

[298] Rick Warren, *The Purpose Driven Life: What on Earth am I here For?*
[299] Psalm 92:5-6 (NAB).

only *we* can discern our true selves and discover our personal *gnothi s'auton*. It is our job and ours alone to do the work necessary to figure out whom God has made us. We go from there, not from any other external source. One of my favorite slogans from twelve-step recovery literature is that "God doesn't make junk." But how often do we give credence to inner voices that tell us we *are* junk? Unfortunately, too often. Those voices were certainly planted there by others, definitely not by God. The number one way to *shine* is to be aware of and to reflect our Creator's built-in design. Remember, that plan was there way before we were on the scene. We each possess a unique purpose built-in to drive us in a positive direction. To discover that direction is to unlock our hidden potential for happiness. These words hold out hope for anyone plagued by a sense of unworthiness to ever lead a purpose-driven life:

> I waited patiently for the Lord;
> he inclined to me and heard my cry.
>
> He drew me up from the desolate pit,
> out of the miry bog,
> and set my feet upon a rock,
> making my steps secure.
>
> He put a new song in my mouth,
> a song of praise to our God.
> Many will see and fear,
> and put their trust in the Lord.[300]

God is on the way to lift me out of my own personal pit, whatever muck or mire might be bogging me down. A helicopter has come to hoist me out of that pit and deposit me on safe ground. Thus rescued, I can imagine myself singing of God's generous grace. Whether we are yet aware

---
300 Psalm 40:1-3.

of our life's purpose or not, one answer to the question *how do we shine?* is modeled by the life of John the Baptist. Shortly before John baptized Jesus, John questioned his first cousin about the virtual "elephant in the room," the obvious role-reversal. "But shouldn't *you* be baptizing *me*?" This encounter reveals one of John's chief virtues, humility. John had his own disciples following him well before Jesus showed up. He too was a rabbi, a teacher, and someone known for holiness of life. John was all prepared, however, for Jesus to arrive on the scene. God had told him that the long-awaited Messiah was about to appear. Another of John's virtues was that he was unthreatened by competition. Rabbis of that day often competed amongst themselves for disciples, for students. Not John the Baptist. His humility, in complete synchronicity with the heart of God, enabled him to recognize and recommend Jesus over himself. John, as often depicted in portraits, would literally point to Jesus as the lamb of God, the one born to pay the ultimate price to redeem humankind:

> John saw Jesus coming toward him and declared, "Here is the Lamb of God who takes away the sin of the world! This is the one of whom I said, 'After me comes a man who ranks ahead of me because he was before me.'"[301]

Because John was older than Jesus, chronologically speaking Jesus *came after* John. But Jesus, being the Eternal Word, the second person of the Trinity, had therefore existed from all eternity. So technically, he existed long before his cousin came on the scene. Key words in the scripture are

---

[301] John 1:29-30. For verse 30, I prefer this version: "He is the one I was talking about when I said, 'A man is coming after me who is far greater than I am, for he existed long before me.'" (NLT) John's reference to the Lamb of God is echoed in the Eucharistic liturgy with the words *Ecce Agnus Dei, ecce qui tollit peccata mundi.*

"who is far greater than me" (NLT) or "who ranks ahead of me" (NRSV). With these words, John especially reveals his humility by admitting he knows why God had created him. He was clear in his own spirit that he was the forerunner of the Messiah, and not the Messiah himself. John graciously sends Andrew and others of his disciples now to become new disciples of his cousin and his Messiah, Jesus of Nazareth. How does John the Baptist shine? Primarily by living a life of humility. He was quite clear about what God expected of him:

> He has told you, O mortal, what is good;
> and what does the Lord require of you
> but to do justice, and to love kindness,
> and to walk humbly with your God?"[302]

The third requirement, humility, was one the Baptist modeled best.

Well, that brings us back to the question "how do *I* shine?" That question requires a three-part answer. First, by *coming to know my true self*, my *gnothi s'auton* discernment exercise. Who did God design me to be? What potentialities had God outlined for me when he brought me into existence? Am I aware of those possible design paths? If I have not yet done my homework in that department, will I actively engage in pursuing those possible paths? Secondly, by *waiting purposely and hopefully*. This is not like my impatiently waiting for a train or a bus that is late and which I doubt will ever arrive. I need to pray about whether hopeful, purposeful waiting is yet a skill set of mine. And third, by *striving for the challenging virtue of humility*. While in our culture humility seems to be a vanishing value, nonetheless an authentic, shining spirituality requires it.

---

302 Micah 6:8.

Shrines

What do you think of when you hear words like *shrine* or *idols*? Many *shrines* have been erected to honor holy women or holy men throughout history. Some are saints, some are just good people who contributed significantly to society. Most of us are familiar with the concept of a shrine, civil or religious in nature, regardless whether we've ever visited one.

At least from a religious standpoint, the word *idol* has a notably negative connotation. But in the parlance of Hollywood, the word *idol* is harmless enough. There are teenage idols, American idols, or just plain movie star idols, you know, the A-listers who make it OTRC, on the Red Carpet. Sometimes, we are said to *idolize* certain people in our lives, those we deeply love, like parents, children, spouses, relatives or our closest friends. But to say that we *idolize* them would be expressing ourselves metaphorically rather than literally.

Idols and their *shrines* were in no sense considered metaphorical in ancient Athens. Paul happens to land there on a missionary journey, and while awaiting his delayed confreres, he takes a self-guided tour around the city. He had time to kill. Paul must have been quite an extrovert. Being intellectually curious, he enjoyed engaging people. He wanted to have a look for himself and see what was going on in this city. And that's where our story begins.[303]

---

303 Acts 17:16-34 *passim*, quoted from *The Message* by Eugene Peterson.

The longer Paul waited in Athens for Silas and Timothy, the angrier he got—all those idols! The city was a junkyard of idols. He discussed it with the Jews and other like-minded people at their meeting place. And every day he went out on the streets and talked with anyone who happened along. He got to know some of the Epicurean and Stoic intellectuals pretty well through these conversations.

Remember, Paul was no peasant. He was a well-educated, upper-crust Jew. He was comfortable among intellectuals or even any pseudo-intellectuals he might encounter around Athens. And as we know, whether dealing with friend or foe, Paul was uncommonly fearless.

Some of them dismissed him with sarcasm: "What an airhead!" But others, listening to him go on about Jesus and the resurrection, were intrigued: "That's a new slant on the gods. Tell us more." Downtown Athens was a great place for gossip. There were always people hanging around, natives and tourists alike, waiting for the latest tidbit on most anything.

And Paul had more than tidbits to offer, more than the latest gossip. After he had engaged a number of people, he was officially invited to address the Athenians in their most hallowed and significant forum.

So, Paul took his stand in the open space at the Areopagus and laid it out for them. "It is plain to see that you Athenians take your religion seriously. When I arrived here the other day, I was fascinated with all the shrines I came across. And then I found one inscribed, to the god nobody knows. I'm here to introduce you to this God so you can worship intelligently, know who you're dealing with.

They had made so many shrines, they'd run out of names! Thus, they had unwittingly left themselves in a vulnerable posture as far as Paul was concerned. Paul saw this as an opportunity to "fill-in-the-blanks." Did someone just forget to inscribe that particular idol or what? Paul let loose on the subject.

> The God who made the world and everything in it, this Master of sky and land, doesn't live in custom-made shrines or need the human race to run errands for him, as if he couldn't take care of himself. He makes the creatures; the creatures don't make him. Starting from scratch, he made the entire human race and made the earth hospitable, with plenty of time and space for living so we could seek after God, and not just grope around in the dark but actually find him. He doesn't play hide-and-seek with us. He's not remote; he's near. We live and move in him, can't get away from him! One of your poets said it well: 'We're the God-created.' Well, if we are the God-created, it doesn't make a lot of sense to think we could hire a sculptor to chisel a god out of stone for us, does it?

He went on to tell the rest of the story, beginning with Jesus' Resurrection and how that had occurred.

> At the phrase "raising him from the dead," the listeners split: Some laughed at him and walked off making jokes; others said, "Let's do this again. We want to hear more." But that was it for the day, and Paul left. There were still others, it

turned out, who were convinced then and there, and stuck with Paul—among them Dionysius the Areopagite and a woman named Damaris.

Peripatetic Paul zeroed in on and seized a wonderful opportunity. In business jargon, there is a certain leadership style known as MBWA or "Management by Walking Around." Rather than sitting comfortably in one's private office, the engaged manager is constantly on the move, circulating, mingling with employees, thereby frequently enabled to take the corporate pulse. The TV series *Undercover Boss* is the ultimate example of MBWA. Perhaps because Paul had time on his hands and was bored, he saw the opportunity to do some evangelical MBWA around Athens. For Paul, however, the "M" would not stand for *management* but for *ministry*. He isn't strolling around Athens as a gaping, gawking tourist, but as a roving pastor, engaging and challenging those he met. Observing, assessing, and networking with anyone he might encounter, Paul is constantly taking their pulse as he spreads the Good News. Paul admitted he was startled at the number of all those *shrines*. Should you travel in Southern Germany and Austria, you will encounter every kind of outdoor *Christian* shrine. All around Athens there were lots of shrines too, but all dedicated to pagan gods. Paul would never encounter Bavaria or the Vienna Woods, but what he was able to see around Athens stunned him.

Invited to address the Athenians, he first complimented them—perhaps with tongue in cheek — on how *religious* they were. They had a god for anything you could ever pray for! But somehow, they had one as yet unnamed shrine left over. Paul used this no-name-shrine as a convenient segue to get his listeners thinking. Greeks were by nature intellectually curious, many honestly searching for their own personal divinity. They sought it the only way they knew how. Paul suggested an *alternative* deity, perhaps the one they had left room for in that nameless shrine. But this would be a God who *was* known, rather than remaining *unknown*, knowable in the person of Jesus Christ. Instead of relying on individual gods, Paul suggested appealing to an overarching, all-purpose God. Paul was offering these seekers another way.

How ironic that the Athenians had actually invited Paul to speak on the *Areopagus*! The *Areopagus* refers to the plain of *Ares*, the Greek god of thunder and war, the equivalent Roman god being *Mars*. The *Areopagus* is sometimes referred to as *Mars Hill*. Paul was preaching about *the One, True God* on the mound in Athens dedicated to one of *many* gods. Paul's secret tool was discerning and seizing a window of opportunity. At a baptism the officiant prays:

> Give them an inquiring and discerning heart, the courage to will and to persevere, a spirit to know and to love you, and the gift of joy and wonder in all your works.[304]

In my own personal MBWA, my *Ministry by Walking Around*, I need to listen for any teachable moment that comes my way, any natural segue within a conversation. It's not my style to stand on a soapbox or thump the Bible, but anyone can speak simply from the heart. John Henry Cardinal Newman, a key figure from the Oxford Movement, chose as his episcopal motto *Cor ad cor loquitur*,[305] illustrated as one heart in dialogue with another. As I walk around my own personal Athens, wherever that might be, am I willing to be on the lookout for any teachable moment? If so, may God help me witness above all that God's love is not only real but steadfast.

---

304 *BCP 1979*, p. 308.
305 Heart speaks to heart.

SILENCE

> Give us grace, O Lord, to answer readily
> the call of our Savior Jesus Christ
> and to proclaim to all people
> the Good News of his salvation.[306]

Those words from an opening collect mention *call* and *proclamation*. And the following words, of such import in the Hebrew Bible, are repeated verbatim in the New Testament:

> The people who sat in darkness have seen
> a great light, and for those who sat in
> the region and shadow of death light has
> dawned.[307]

What is *darkness*? What is *light*? And precisely what *call* might we be asked to *answer readily*? In the classic film *The Graduate*,[308] "The Sound of Silence"[309] was a prominently recurring theme song expressing the leitmotiv of the story. The words of that song address us in terms of this meditation when they begin with "Hello darkness, my old friend" and end with "the sound of silence."

Why, for many of us, is darkness considered to be *our*

---

306 *BCP 1979*, p. 215.
307 Isaiah 9:2 and Matthew 4:16.
308 A romantic comedy-drama directed by Mike Nichols (1967).
309 Simon and Garfunkel (1964).

old friend? For the young graduate in that film, darkness had indeed been his old friend, his constant companion for many years. Perhaps it was the darkness of a blank slate, a *tabula rasa.* Perhaps throughout college he was so focused on his studies that he allowed himself no time for meaningful human relationships. Perhaps he was a victim of his own silence, that reluctance to communicate with others on any authentic level of self-disclosure. But in any case, after graduation something had changed for young Benjamin. While sleeping, he experiences a vision which became *planted within his brain.* Perhaps initially that vision might have been awakened by the seductive Mrs. Robinson. But Benjamin's vision—for good or for ill—was not to end there. It would eventually bear fruit in something far more wholesome. He would engage in a genuine human relationship with her daughter, Elaine.

A strange way for anyone to become awakened! A strange way to come alive to a wholesome human relationship. But nonetheless, it was Benjamin's way. For him, darkness had given way to light. His *tabula rasa*, his blank slate, for so many years suspended in dormancy, had now suddenly become filled with all kinds of written messages. These were neither scribble nor scrawl but coherent sentences, something he could *read, mark, learn, and inwardly digest,* make some sense out of, and ultimately, have the courage of his conviction to follow.

From time to time, each of us inhabits his or her own brand of *silence,* that nothingness of darkness, our own personal *tabula rasa,* a whiteboard so pristine that nothing has even been scribbled on it. It doesn't even reveal an erasure. This may be our very moment to change that, to put something up on our blank whiteboard, if even only a rough draft. It might be an outline to be fleshed-out, only later to become incarnate. But at least we put *something* up there for now, if only a sketch, if only a start. What good is a brand-new whiteboard if we never use it?

> Give us grace, O Lord, to answer readily
> the call of our Savior Jesus Christ
> and to proclaim to all people
> the Good News of his salvation.[310]

Are we prepared to respond to such grace, should it be given us? Imagine you have just been gifted with your own, brand-new, right out-of-the-shipping box, blank whiteboard. Why not make use it right away to draft a personal mission statement? Remember, the operative word is *draft*. God expects we'll revise it from time to time. How about starting with this goal: "to proclaim to all people the Good News of God's salvation?" But little old me? Just how might I accomplish such a lofty objective? That's something for clergy professionals, isn't it?

Well, I'm afraid not. That excuse doesn't hold water. The apostles, the disciples of Jesus were anything but trained professionals. Jesus called ordinary, uneducated manual laborers attracted by his magnetism and open to seeking truth. That collect does pose a challenge. It asks you to ponder significant life-questions: "how can I break the sound barrier of silence in my own spiritual life?" How can I cast off darkness and embrace light, write on the blank, unused slate of my life, and migrate from silence into sound? The closing verse of *The Sound of Silence* puts it beautifully. That final verse refers to the *Ersatz* gods we create, the shinier, the glitzier, the flashier, the better. It's recounting all the false starts, seductive encounters, and unproductive relationships we have embraced, all those other *strange gods*[311] who

---

310 *BCP 1979*, p. 215.
311 Exodus 20:2-3. I am the Lord thy God, who brought thee out of the land of Egypt, out of the house of bondage. Thou shalt not have strange gods before me.

constantly compete for our attention. But let's not criticize. These are, after all, only *drafts* people have scribbled on their whiteboards. At least they *tried* to engage life, to interact, albeit in a misguided and fruitless way.

When you and I attempt to break out of our darkness, choose sound over silence to fill our void, sometimes we do choose *neon gods*, false deities. We become deluded into thinking these look-alikes will make something happen for us. But false gods are *strange gods*, foreign entities who cannot produce. This neon sign, however, flashed a worthwhile and truthful message:

Ah, "the words of the prophets." The kind of exalted wisdom I have read on the pages of my bible doesn't even come close to what I find scrawled on subway walls and tenement halls, and whispered—if ever so subtly—*in the sound of silence*. What a useful tool silence can be in our spiritual toolkit! Within that elusive realm known as *the sound of silence*, I can both discern as well as answer God's call. Help me stop, look, and listen, dear Lord, but above all listen!

SNAKES

Unless you suffer from *achromatopsia* or color-blindness, when you visit a liturgical church you will notice a distinct feature, namely how they use different colors. Starting off with purple or blue on the first Sunday of Advent and ending up with white or gold on the last Sunday after Pentecost, you will have witnessed a grand display of the liturgical colors for church seasons and festivals. This is a feature which goes to the heart of the Catholic heritage of Anglicanism. A chief characteristic of Catholic worship is to involve as many of the five senses as possible. We see colors, we hear music, words and preaching, we taste the Communion wine and wafers, we smell the fragrance of incense, and feel the touch of another at the exchange of peace.

The use of eight distinct liturgical colors[312] appeals strongly to our visual sense. On the Fourth Sunday in Lent, for example, the celebrant may choose rose instead of violet. That is perhaps the most striking color change since it occurs only two Sundays each year.[313] If you have a look at the scriptures selected for the fourth Sunday in Lent, you will discover that each one points us in the direction of hope. Lest we dwell too intensely on past transgressions and plunge too deeply into sorrow for sin, a mid-season Sunday "in the pink" is there to lift us, as the Latin proverb says, *per*

---

312 White, gold, violet, rose, blue, red, green and black.
313 The third Sunday in Advent and the fourth Sunday in Lent.

aspera ad astra, through trials to triumph, through hard times to heaven. Several educational institutions have adopted these very words as their school motto and displayed them on an official seal. A Rose Sunday, if even for a day, invites us to espy and reach for the *astra*, the stars of triumph. Even if we haven't begun to journey quite that far, nor have arrived there yet, we are still reminded that we are *in via*, on our way, and encouraged to remain there on that heavenward journey.

Where does the theme *per aspera ad astra* show up in Rose Sunday scriptures? In the Hebrew Bible, the Book of Numbers recounts the *aspera* Israelites had to endure on their challenging journey. It reveals their impatience with the lack of amenities Moses provided. They grumble about everything: the dearth of water, the substandard food, and how much they miss the good old days:

> The people became impatient on the way. They spoke against God and against Moses, "Why have you brought us up out of Egypt to die in the wilderness? For there is no food and no water, and we detest this miserable food."[314]

God is not at all pleased with their ungratefulness, nor should he be. So, what does God do? He doesn't send amenities, he sends snakes. And we all know what snakes do, right? They bite:

> They bit the people, so that many Israelites died.[315]

But eventually the Israelites repented of their bad behavior, turned themselves around, turned over a new leaf, and showed their contrition:

---

314 Numbers 21:4-5.
315 Numbers 21:6.

> The people came to Moses and said, "We have sinned by speaking against the LORD and against you; pray to the LORD to take away the serpents from us." So Moses prayed for the people.³¹⁶

Their version of a Rose Sunday half-time came in the form of a most unorthodox solution to their snake problem:

> And the LORD said to Moses, "Make a poisonous serpent, and set it on a pole; and everyone who is bitten shall look at it and live." So Moses made a serpent of bronze, and put it upon a pole; and whenever a serpent bit someone, that person would look at the serpent of bronze and live.³¹⁷

Thus, the God who loved them so dearly inspires his servant Moses to find a creative way to shed some rays of light along their seemingly endless dark tunnel of pilgrimage. God invents a solution to the same problem he created. God turns the snake, a symbol of death, into a source of healing. The *Caduceus* is the insignia for the medical profession. Physicians frequently used to display it above their license plate to get a better parking spot and in hopes of avoiding a ticket. This mythological symbol known as a *Caduceus* showed two snakes wrapped around a single wand. Legend had it that the wand had the power to wake the sleeping and to send those awake to sleep. If applied to the dying, they would experience a gentle death; if applied to the dead, they would come back to life.

The snake of the Hebrew Bible prefigured what Jesus would endure in his passion and death on the Cross. The

---
316 Numbers 21:7.
317 Numbers 21:8-9.

hard wood of the Cross, the tree of death, would become for us the tree of life, because "God so loved the world."[318] The snake Moses would lift up on his staff meant neither condemnation nor punishment for the disobedient, but was rather a signpost for healing. In the same way, Christ would not be lifted up upon a cross to die forever like a common criminal but rather to become the ultimate healer of our wounded world, the world he so loved. In the desert, the serpent was lifted up to heal the Israelites. On the cross, Christ Jesus would be lifted up to draw all of us, even little old me, unto himself... for "by his wounds we are healed."[319]

---

[318] John 3:16.
[319] 1 Peter 2:24: He himself bore our sins in his body on the cross, so that, free from sins, we might live for righteousness; by his wounds you have been healed.

Stewardship

There used to be a very common expression when someone felt the urge to give their unsolicited opinion on something. The person would jump into the conversation and say, "If I may put *my* two cents in," or in other words, "I am about to offer my opinion, for whatever it's worth. Two cents doesn't buy much these days, so my opinion may be worth very little."

But how does one define *very little*? Once I was in the sacristy of a parish I served, preparing to celebrate Mass, and I actually found two copper pennies lying on the vesting table. Later that week, at the grocery store I got another two cents back in change. These coincidences made me think about that story from the twelfth chapter of Mark's Gospel where a poor widow drops her "two small copper coins, worth a penny" into the collection plate.

The actual cash value of that contribution was even back then worth next to *nada*. But it was all the poor woman had. Mark talks about the scribes, those establishment fat cats who loved to strut around in all their finery, take the best seats in the house, and recite long, tedious prayers. They probably could have easily contributed sums far larger than two cents. But did they? Would they?

As Jesus pointed out, these individuals *devour widows' houses*. Today that would translate as foreclosure for defaulting on a mortgage. There are still among us the uber-rich who wouldn't bat an eyelash at turning impoverished widows into street people. Yet the same individuals would dare to put on a sanctimonious Sabbath front and make sure everybody knew how "sacrificial" their pledge was. These were by no means your *anonymous donors*.

One collect identifies Jesus' mission as "coming into the world that he might destroy the works of the devil," and asks that we may "purify ourselves as he is pure." So the basic question is: are we doing God's work or the devil's? Are we giving out of our abundance or out of however little we have?

If you compare the Book of Ruth with the parable of the poor widow, answer this question for yourself: whose work was Ruth doing? What prompted her to stay with her mother-in-law? And what motivated the impoverished widow to part with her last red cent?

Diabolical works, satanic strategies or just plain devilish doings are the polar opposites of the godly works of the *pure in heart*. The beatitudes say "Blessed are the pure in heart, for they shall see God."[320] The pure in heart strive daily to become more godly, more God-like. Becoming pure in heart doesn't happen by itself but is part of the spiritual pilgrimage.

The devilish doings of scribal behavior did not happen overnight either, but were rather born of a lifelong lifestyle of social injustice. Somehow, a mean, stingy, self-promotional worldview does not improve with time. It only gets worse. Ultimately, their attitude led to Jesus' crucifixion. A prideful, scornful, and self-congratulatory attitude only festers and intensifies.

In sharp contrast, Ruth opts to stay by her mother-in-law Naomi even after her husband, Naomi's son, had died. What an exceptional random act of self-sacrifice! Ruth was under absolutely no obligation to stay behind with Naomi. She would have been free to go pursue her own self-interest.

---

[320] Matthew 5:1-12.

But that's not who Ruth was. Ruth declared: "Whither thou goest, I will go." For such an extraordinary sacrifice she was blessed with a new husband in Boaz, and ultimately Ruth became David's great-grandmother, thus beginning the line of David. Through her selfless generosity Ruth would become an ancestor of Jesus himself through his foster father, Joseph. Virtue is indeed its own often-unexpected reward. Some sow, others reap, and virtue begets virtue.

Undoubtedly, the poor widow had likewise suffered the slings and arrows of misfortune. Her husband having died, she now had no further source of income. The bank, as it were, had foreclosed on her home (they devour widows' houses). She was virtually *penniless*, but not quite. She trusted God and gave whatever she had left back to God. By so doing, she literally put in her *last* two cents. For her, that was it. That was all she had. From an establishment viewpoint, from human rather than divine perspective, her offering was meaningless. Just one more thing for the wealthy to scoff at, to discount rather than to honor the heroism of her gift.

That poor woman reminds me of the widow of Zarephath.[321] While traveling, the prophet Elijah one day stopped at her house and asked her for food. She fed him, although that would mean both she and her son would have no more to eat. She too trusted God to provide and was blessed for her generosity. Because she fed Elijah, they would never run out of food again. Her single act of radical trust set a miracle in motion. Ruth took a similar leap of faith, one coupled with much love, when she opted to stay back with Naomi, rather than pursue her own future. All three: Ruth, the widow in the Temple, and the widow of Zarephath each opted to do the *right* thing rather than the *smart* thing. One virtuous act can set in motion a chain of blessings, as

---

321 1 Kings 17:10.

it did when you consider the ancestry line set in motion by Ruth's extraordinary generosity: the "line of David" might never have existed, had it not been for Ruth's loyalty so many centuries before.

Ruth → Naomi → Boaz → David → Joseph → Jesus

The rich young man who asked Jesus what his next step toward perfection should be was unprepared to embrace *radical dispossession*.[322] Ruth *was* willing, as were both impoverished widows. Their unmitigated generosity did not go unnoticed by the Lord. Rather than becoming destitute, they were rewarded for purity of heart and generosity of soul.

May these biblical profiles in courage motivate us to abandon the fear of loss. May we learn from such heroic women fearlessly and cheerfully to contribute whatever we can offer to usher in the Kingdom of God.

---

[322] Mark 10: 17-31.

Strangers

> Do not fail to show love to strangers,
> for by doing this some have welcomed
> angels without realizing it.[323]

"Hey, come on, you guys! It's me!" Jesus definitely did *not* say this to the group walking along beside him on the road to Emmaus. He probably wanted to but he held back. He was having too much fun. He didn't want to spoil his disciples' surprise when they actually discovered who the stranger in their midst was, walking right beside them. Whether or not he was aware of it, Jesus was employing what rhetoricians would later term *the Socratic method*. Socrates would go around ancient Athens posing all sorts of philosophical questions. He wanted to get people thinking about issues and coming up with their own answers rather than giving the answers away himself.

Although they were all going along this same road together, they were all at various places in their own spiritual walk. They had questions. They had hopes. Or at least, up till now they had had hope. Naturally, they had become depressed at the unfortunate turn of events. Things hadn't worked out at all as they had anticipated. What catastrophe was about to befall them next? Would Jesus ever reappear? Where was he now? Was he dead or alive? Lots of questions.

---

323 Hebrews 13:2 (EHV).

Lots of worries, fears. But the trek to Emmaus gave them time to talk but with no apparent resolution. At any rate, here they all were, walking along, kicking up dust with one another on the road to Emmaus. All of a sudden, they are joined by someone totally unfamiliar to them, some stranger—at least that's what they thought. These disappointed disciples were so totally self-absorbed in their own uncertainty, so completely preoccupied with their own future that they were unprepared for some unknown person to show up and crash their scene. Here comes along this stranger out of nowhere. He seemed completely clueless about the recent, literally earth-shaking events. His ignorance only heightened their anxiety and increased their annoyance at his uncalled-for intrusion.

"Are you the only person who is completely ignorant about recent current events here?" The stranger's purported cluelessness ultimately cleared the way for Jesus to seize a teachable moment. Although annoyed by his staged naivete, the disciples were therefore obliged to recount the recent events in painstaking detail. By feigning ignorance, Jesus was able to give them an opportunity to debrief as well as witness. For the disciples, this served as both a therapeutic *and* a kerygmatic moment. Because this stranger was supposedly so totally uninformed, telling the story boosted their own morale and gave them an opportunity to evangelize. In his numerous post-Resurrection encounters, Jesus invites his disciples to recognize him. Each encounter serves its own specific purpose. In this encounter, Jesus as it were plays dumb. He baits these confused disciples so that they'll open up and share what's on their hearts. He provides a mechanism to relieve much of their pent-up anger, anxiety, diffidence, and confusion about his fate in particular and about Resurrection life in general.

How do you and I treat *strangers*? How do I interact

with someone I don't know or at least don't know well? The word *strange* has multiple connotations. A *strange* person can mean that they are *foreign*, whether foreign-born, of foreign descent, someone coming from a different part of the country or the world, or just somebody who is *different*. A *strange* person can mean that they are *odd*, maybe even *weird*. When I encounter someone new, do I immediately take a like or a dislike to them based on how they look? Or do I intentionally look past all that and try to take a deeper look, into their soul? After he had interviewed a goodly number of far more likely candidates, Samuel discovered David last. Although the youngest and least likely of all Jesse's sons, still young David was the man God had chosen. But the prophet Samuel had to make an effort to look past these externals, to go beneath the superficial, to go deeper.[324] Do I know who the stranger is in our midst? Do I really know who's walking right along beside me?

---

[324] 1 Samuel 16:7. "But the Lord said to Samuel, 'Do not look on his appearance or on the height of his stature, because I have rejected him; for the Lord does not see as mortals see; they look on the outward appearance, but the Lord looks on the heart.'" See also Isaiah 11:3 "Not by appearance shall he judge, nor by hearsay shall he decide."

TRANSFIGURATION

The liturgical calendar actually celebrates the Transfiguration of Jesus twice: first, on the last Sunday after Epiphany; and then on its own proper feast, August 6th. What is so significant about this event that it warrants two feast days? Exactly what happened on that mountaintop to merit such special attention? The account is also recorded in all three synoptic gospels[325] which alone would call attention to it. But why? Isn't this just one more mountaintop scene, one more peak experience? Instead, why not emphasize the more down-to-earth kind of plain talk we are used to hearing from Jesus? How about some straight-from-the-shoulder messages about non-violent resistance, turning the other cheek, or loving your enemies?[326]

The Transfiguration of Jesus sends an altogether different kind of message. It is a mystical experience involving major players in the Divine drama: *God* the Creator, *Jesus* the Messiah, *Peter* the prime apostle, *John*, undeniably Jesus' "favorite" apostle, along with his brother *James*, not to mention significant cameo appearances by *Moses* and *Elijah*. Truly, this was a gathering of eagles, an assembly of biblical giants. But on a more personal plane, where are *we* in this drama? Where could we see ourselves in this spectacular event? How can we at least place ourselves virtually there in that transfiguration drama and experience it vicariously?

---

325   Matthew 17:1-9; Mark 9:2-9; Luke 9:28-36.
326   Matthew 5:38-48.

Reality TV understands mystery but does not get mysticism. Ironically, Reality TV doesn't represent true reality at all. Contemporary media culture would dismiss any mystical experience as kookiness or craziness. But to enter into mystical experience, searching for the *unio mystica*,[327] is the reality of coming home to our true selves. There we discover God the ever-immanent *Emmanuel* already present and dwelling within us.

In the following meditation, I hope you might be game for something a little different. If you would like to join me on a virtual journey, I'd ask you to please take a few moments now to quiet your heart before embarking on a little trip.

Imagine right now that Jesus has just texted you. Jesus has invited a few of us to accompany him mountain climbing along with Peter, James, and John. It's not Mt Everest, no worries, just a gentle slope on a nice sunny afternoon. You and I are invited, and despite our questionable athletic prowess, we say "yes, sure we'll go along." After all, it *is* Jesus who's inviting us. Who could refuse? We don't really get why he is including *us* along with such gospel greats, but we'll show up and see anyway. Along the way up the mountain, we exchange chitchat. The grade up this hill isn't all that steep, thank God; there are places to stop and catch our breath, sip some bottled water, maybe munch on an energy bar.

After about a half hour's walk we get to the summit. The view is spectacular. We can see for miles in all directions. The weather is near perfect. Not a cloud in the sky. We begin to experience a peculiar peace we have never known before. This is a *special* time, a *special* space. We sense an indefinable peace emanating from Jesus. Our other fellow hikers are neat traveling companions, but somehow Jesus stands out from the others. He starts praying; and invites us to pray along

---

327 The mystical union with God was the pearl of great price sought by many mystics such as Meister Eckhart, Teresa of Avila and St. John of the Cross.

with him. Slowly he pronounces the Lord's Prayer, addressing his own Dad. As we are praying together, Jesus' appearance gradually starts to change. His somewhat perspiration-soiled clothing after hiking up the hill suddenly turns dazzling, sparkling white. His no longer sweaty face begins to shine, to radiate light.

Suddenly, two other men appear, one on his left and the other on his right, neither of whom had been on the hike with us. They seem to have virtually come out of nowhere. Soon we make out the familiar figures of Moses and Elijah. They stand there conversing with Jesus about what lies before him in Jerusalem. They are discussing his impending passion and death. At this crucial moment, you and I are very much awake, very much aware of what is happening and what is being said. But Peter, James, and John, somewhat exhausted from the hike, are napping. As they finally wake up, Moses and Elijah have just about concluded speaking with Jesus and are ready to depart. Barely half-awake, Peter typically blurts out something. He suggests they build there three structures, one for Jesus, one for Moses, and one for Elijah.

At this point, right now, *you* are just about ready to say something. *You* enter the scene and engage in the conversation. Everyone is still present. Our Old Testament figures have yet to depart, so that they, as well as Peter, James, John, along with Jesus, will be able to hear whatever you have to say. But what do you *want* to say? This is your chance to engage. What is on your heart right now, after seeing what you have seen and hearing what you have heard? You can make those comments silently in your heart, maybe say them out loud, or journal on them. In any case, take your time. There is no rush. The others will wait and listen. At a mystical moment such as this, we all might have something very personal to say, and now is the hour.

All right, you have now finished saying what you wanted

to. Suddenly, a massive, threatening cloud arrives on the scene. Up till that point it had been so very bright and sunny. But now suddenly this thick, dark cloud comes out of nowhere and obscures everyone. Understandably, you're somewhat surprised, perhaps even alarmed at this sudden change in weather. What could it possibly portend? But you are immediately reassured when you hear the Father softly and tenderly pronounce these familiar words:

> This is the Son I chose. This is the child I love.
> Listen to what he has to say, and from now on
> listen to him only.

Suddenly you become aware that Moses and Elijah aren't there anymore, only Jesus. Your experience on that mountain peak lingers because it has been so personal, so real, and so overwhelming. Now, the trek back down to level ground, *terra firma*, but no more idle chatter is heard. You return in total silence. Something profound has happened to you and to your hiking companions and you want to preserve that "peace that passes all understanding" and never let it go. As an active participant you have personally tasted the *unio mystica*. No passive spectator, you responded to those mystical moments in your own words, speaking from the heart, a memory you will cherish forever. And you will recall that God is love and that love transfigures, heals and ultimately wins, despite whatever clouds may seem to overshadow joy.

Truth

What *is* truth? What do you *mean* by it? Are there various *versions* of the truth? Why in court proceedings do they make you swear or affirm to "tell the truth, the whole truth, and nothing but the truth?" And why is there always such a severe penalty for perjury, for lying under oath? All important questions yet for some, unanswered questions, or at least unsatisfactorily answered questions.

In the section of the Passion narrative where Jesus is dragged before Pilate,[328] Pilate utters perhaps his most significant line. He carries on a protracted dialogue with Jesus whom he really does not want to execute, whom he finds innocent of any capital offense, and yet whom he cannot understand. After Jesus describes that his life's mission has been to bring about truth, Pilate's only rejoinder is "What is truth?" One translation renders it this way: "'Truth,' said Pilate. 'What's that?'"[329] To put it even more colloquially but accurately: "What do you *mean* by truth?"

Pilate's response to "What do you *mean* by truth?" might have admitted of *alternative facts*, as a politician once put it. Or Pilate might have claimed that he always told *some version* of the truth.[330] But facts have no *alternatives*, and truth has no *versions*. And to qualify as *truth* it must include

---

328 John 18: 28-38.
329 John 18: 38 (NTE).
330 As Jack Nicholson explained to Diane Keaton in the film *Something's Gotta Give* (2003).

the whole truth, and nothing but. Pilate's tone was likely sarcastic, scornful, and contemptuous of Jesus and his entire philosophy. Pilate could only see Jesus as a political rival someone the higher-ups in his chain of command would not appreciate. Jesus, a Jew, amounted to nothing but a nuisance and distraction for Pilate and the rest of the Roman occupation. Pilate's cynical but crucial question about the meaning of truth marks a turning point in their dialogue. The question likewise addresses you and me.

The theological thrust of Pilate's question provided Rabbi Jesus with a teachable moment. Pilate had garnered various bits of the truth about Jesus, but had remained skeptical about the very *existence* of truth itself. His cynicism blinded him from putting the pieces together in the person of Jesus now standing before him. His skepticism, stubbornness, and entitled status blinded him from connecting the dots. Unfortunately, these impediments sidetracked and ultimately derailed Pilate from ever comprehending the meaning of *truth*.

The question "What is truth?" cannot be adequately addressed without at least a mustard seed of faith. St. Anselm sorted out the proverbial "chicken or the egg" conundrum in his proposition *fides quaerens intellectum,* faith seeks understanding. Anselm said that faith comes first. Even a scant scintilla of *faith* can lead me to some *understanding* of religion. One Jesuit university expresses the same principle in their motto *Per fidem ad plenam veritatem,*[331] through faith to full truth. If I should start to stagnate in skeptical agnosticism, faith has the ability to jump start my journey toward truth. Having to deal with the prisoner Jesus, Pilate was in no frame of mind to think through what Jesus was saying much less explore it. After all, Jesus was a Jewish problem not a Roman

---

331   The registered trademark of Fairfield University, founded in 1942.

one. The Messiah issue was just one more annoyance to a middle-management bureaucrat who considered himself a rising star. He hadn't the foggiest notion what Jesus was talking about nor did he at all care, as Jesus tried to explain:

> "For this I was born, and for this I have come into the world, to bear witness to the truth. Everyone who is of the truth hears my voice."[332]

The only response Pilate could make to Jesus' mission statement was to fire back that petulant, cynical counter-question "What is truth? What do you mean by that?" His tone was dismissive of its very existence. He might as well have put it this way: "Truth? What the heck is that? What value could truth possibly have?" The *red thread*[333] in any literary genre refers to a consistent theme running through it. The red thread running through the entire New Testament could be summed up in one word, truth. From the promised Messiah of the Hebrew Bible to a resurrected Christ in the New Testament, we see the red thread of truth finally coming to fulfillment. The whole cloth fabric of salvation history is richly embroidered with such red silk threads of truth, carefully woven in seamless fashion from expectation to fulfillment.

The potentially fruitful dialog between Pilate and Jesus breaks down with Pilate's malicious question, *what is truth?* Suddenly, Jesus falls silent. He refuses to engage Pilate any further in fruitless debate. This question ended the conversation. Pilate was constitutionally unable to grasp the concept of truth. When you or I discount, discredit or dilute truth, dialog with our Lord likewise breaks down.

---

332 John 18:37.
333 German scholarship identifies the leitmotiv in a literary work as *der rote Faden*.

Well, to Pilate I would like to say this: "Finally, here is your truth. Acknowledge it: *He has risen as He said!* That is incontrovertible truth and our final answer to your jaded question arising from your sad existentialist lament. See at last the true red thread you refused to recognize."

God is always faithful to God's promises. God always provides unconditionally, regardless how far we might have wandered. The Establishment couldn't understand what Jesus meant by "Destroy this temple and in three days I will rebuild it."[334] Even the Gospel writer felt obliged to elaborate. But now you and I have just seen Truth speaking for itself. As Easter people, we witness to the truth. Our faith, however miniscule, has sought and finally found some modicum of understanding. The temple has been renovated and rebuilt, and it's better than new.

---

334 John 2:19.

Understanding

> I have not stopped thanking God for you. I pray for you constantly, asking God, the glorious Father of our Lord Jesus Christ, to give you spiritual wisdom and insight so that you might grow in your knowledge of God. I pray that your hearts will be flooded with light so that you can understand the confident hope he has given to those he called—his holy people who are his rich and glorious inheritance.[335]

The Seven Gifts of the Holy Spirit are Wisdom, Understanding, Counsel, Fortitude, Knowledge, Piety, and Fear of the Lord.[336] Wisdom, understanding, and knowledge are often confused with one another. It is important at the outset to sort these out and distinguish *understanding* as essentially different from the related gifts of *wisdom* and *knowledge*.

1. **Wisdom (*sapientia*)** Rather than being an encyclopedia of facts, wisdom is the gift that allows an individual to recognize truth. A person with wisdom is able to sort things out and separate fact from fiction, truth from falsehood.

---

335 Ephesians 1:16-18 (NLT).
336 Isaiah 11:2 is the initial biblical reference.

2. **Understanding (*intellectus*)** Understanding, as the Latin indicates, has to do with the intellect. How does it differ from wisdom? While wisdom does the initial, rough-screening of data, intellectual understanding penetrates deeper, to grasp the message beneath the words. Understanding allows one to grasp the *deep structure*[337] of an occurrence rather than simply its surface structure.

3. **Knowledge (*cognitio*)** Knowledge, as the Latin indicates, has to do with cognition, and the related word recognition. It implies being familiar with something or someone, rather than simply being able to research and recite a string of disembodied facts. People who *know* something or someone are *convinced* about their encounter with them.

"For as yet they did not understand the scripture, that he must rise from the dead."[338] A close reading of John's account of Easter morning reveals a story centered on a tomb. Everyone seems to be either on their way *towards* or *away from* the tomb, the primary place of dialog. Mary Magdalene is both the first and last character in this event. And aside from the writer himself, John the Beloved, she is clearly central to this extraordinary event, indeed the pivotal one of salvation history. Peter, the so-called *rock*, does not often receive favorable press in the Gospels. Once again, he is here portrayed as typically lethargic, slow-moving, low-energy, slow-witted, and stodgy. Not until a good deal later in Acts will we witness his emboldened, passionate conviction. At the tomb, Peter is still quite clueless. He would seem to lack *understanding* of what had just transpired.

But most apostles all still remained in the dark. Twice

---

337 A term first coined by linguist Noam Chomsky.
338 John 20:9.

while at the tomb, a key question is put to Mary Magdalene. Arguably the most energetic, motivated seeker of Jesus, she was the disciple most transformed by him. If anyone were really able to understand who this man Jesus was, that would be Mary. But she was asked two questions, "Woman, why are you weeping?" and then, "Who are you looking for?" Luke's account pushes the envelope further: "Why are you looking for the living among the dead?" That rhetorical question answers itself. She is looking for Jesus in the wrong place, sharing the misguided notion that her beloved *Yeshua* is deceased and entombed, and that's it.

It would take the disciples the entire fifty days of Easter to finally get what Resurrection Life meant. Not only before death but afterwards, Jesus remained patient and long-suffering with the motley crew he had cobbled together. His followers were average people like you and me. They would struggle with questions of life after death, or better, life after life.[339] They still somehow clung to the notion that cross and tomb spelled the end. A faint, nostalgic memory might linger, much like annual memorial tributes published in newspapers. These notices recall deceased people whose memory we wish to keep alive.

Remembering Jesus that way was about all many had hoped for. Yet during Eastertide, "the great fifty days after Easter," is when Jesus stayed to walk, talk, and teach his disciples, so you and I might better *understand*—might finally comprehend. Jesus, the Ultimate Teacher, was all about making sure we grasped the truth.

The only one who really got it right Easter morning was Mary Magdalene. Towards the end of her dialog with Jesus, she moves to embrace him. Once she finds out he is no gardener or flunky, nor even some angel but the God-man

---

339 See Raymond A. Moody, MD, *Life after Life*.

she adores, she finds it impossible to keep her distance. As she is about to throw her arms around Jesus, hug him tight, and hold him close, ecstatically joyful that he is really alive, that "he has risen, as he said," Jesus bids her tenderly, "Do not cling to me, do not hold on to me." Their relationship would not end in that tomb. Jesus and Mary Magdalene still had literally *crucial* work to do, the continuing work of the *cross*. She must go and inform the reticent male disciples. She had now gotten her first apostolic commission: to be first to testify to the Resurrection!

And now without delay, Jesus must begin remedial education. Rabbi *Yeshua* must now conduct endless review sessions assuring that his pupils, the disciples, *understood*. Jesus had to be convinced that they really *got* all the lessons he had been preaching. This would be crucial for Jesus to know. Otherwise, would he ever feel confident enough to depart from his church on earth? He must be persuaded that God's house was indeed *built upon a rock* and sustainable going forward. When he was finally convinced that they *understood*, only then would Jesus feel comfortable enough to ascend to his Father and finally go home.

Which characters do you and I get to play in this pivotal drama? Where might I hide out when the going gets tough? Am I just wasting time rummaging around, looking for the living among the dead? How can I ever expect to find life where only its opposite exists? Like Mary Magdalen, do I eagerly run joyfully expecting our Lord? Or am I mostly sauntering along, halfway convinced that all this is but a fruitless exercise? Are spiritual exercises only a waste of time? Do I sometimes wonder whether Jesus is dead and gone? Am I erring about, "looking for love in all the wrong places," lingering in tombs where no life can be found?

Or hopefully, do you and I aspire to be more like St. Mary Magdalene: energetic, persistent, and pro-active? Remember: she was the one who loved much because she had sinned much and was most generously forgiven. Mary proclaimed to her anxiety-ridden brothers: "I have seen the Lord." She identified exactly whom she had found. Would I be bold enough to repeat her words, "I have seen the Lord" to friends and neighbors, and mean it? Identifying with the Magdalene, do I believe that though I *have sinned much*, yet God is just as ready to forgive me as he was Mary?

Unexpected

I like bumper stickers. While I keep my own car as inconspicuous as possible, I do enjoy reading what's plastered all over other people's bumpers. They always tell a story. One bumper sticker I enjoyed seeing said *Expect a Miracle*. Maybe these drivers are only lobbying for a minor miracle such as finding a good parking place or not getting stuck in traffic. What I like about that message is that it expresses optimism, hopefulness. It anticipates the unanticipated, it searches for a four-leaf clover amidst the endless lawns of life. To expect a miracle is to hope for some extraordinary blessing to crop up and surprise us as we live our rather routine, insignificant, or God forbid, toxic lives. When you routinely greet someone with "How's it going?" how often do they respond "Not too bad"? That's as much as saying "I'm making it alright, but just barely." We seldom expect anything stupendous to happen, least of all a miracle.

An elderly couple, *Sarai* and *Abram*, get their names changed to *Sarah* and *Abraham* because the Lord has an unlikely mission for them.[340] God is calling them to become co-creators with him and the parents of many. On entering a religious order, at investiture the new monk or nun receives not only a habit but also a new first name. The superior, abbot or abbess, prior or prioress, renames the person. Bestowing a new identity signifies a new mission. At their advanced age, Abraham and Sarah were stunned that God would call

---

340 Genesis 17:1-7, 15-16.

upon them to do anything, least of all to repopulate the world. But regardless of a seemingly impossible assignment, they stepped forward in faith and their mission was actually accomplished.

> Hoping against hope, [Abraham] believed that he would become "the father of many nations," according to what was said, "So numerous shall your descendants be."[341]

Faith, hope, and love are referred to as the three *theological virtues*. It is interesting to observe the interplay among these virtues. Abraham's *faith* led him to *hope* against all hope. And his *faith* and *hope* together triggered his response, the *love* of God. He loved God so much that he obeyed without debate or hesitation. Biblical stories continue to witness further instances of Abrahamic faith. But it all began with a simple mustard seed of faith planted in the ground as soon as God called. Surprising results usually follow a display of deep faith. Not all Gospel figures responded as promptly or assuredly as did these two aged saints. The Gospels abound in examples of Peter's impetuosity tempered by Jesus' ability to use his less-desirable traits for a teachable moment. A prime example of this may be seen at Jesus' first prediction of his passion and death. Peter won't hear it. Another example occurs at Jesus' arrest when an angry Peter impetuously slices off a soldier's ear. Peter shoots from the hip and Jesus calls him on such impulsive behavior:

> But he turned and said to Peter, "Get behind me, Satan! You are a stumbling-block to me; for you are setting your mind not on divine things but on human things."[342]

---

341 Romans 4:18.
342 Matthew 16:23.

Human reckoning versus divine calibration! Peter is surprised to hear such a harsh rebuke from the master. Being called *Satan* is no compliment. Getting *behind* Jesus doesn't refer to being a supporter either but means "Get out of my sight!" This is an unexpected cold shower for such a good-natured but hot-blooded character as Peter. The teaching moment follows:

> For those who want to save their life will
> lose it, and those who lose their life for
> my sake, and for the sake of the gospel,
> will save it.[343]

Peter was trying to *save his life*, and Jesus' life as well. He was hell-bent on preserving the status quo, allowing for no bumps in the road ahead. Jesus confronted Peter with the Gospel paradox, the seeming contradiction of the normally expected. *Expect the Unexpected* would be another great bumper sticker for our spiritual pilgrimage. Peter never anticipated hearing Jesus' grim but honest prediction about his suffering and death to come. He never expected Jesus' extreme rebuke for his wrongheaded response. Peter had as yet not understood that losing one's life means gaining one's life, eternal life, that is.

Another example of expecting the unexpected may be seen in this collect:

> Be gracious to all who have gone astray
> from your ways, and bring them again
> with penitent hearts and steadfast faith
> to embrace and hold fast
> the unchangeable truth of your Word.[344]

---

343 Mark 8:35.
344 *BCP 1979*, p. 218 (Collect for Second Sunday in Lent).

This prayer is for those who have gotten onto the wrong path. It expresses confidence that God's grace can get them back on track and keep them there. Many who have gone down a wrong path simply stay there, without a clue how to head back in the right direction. It's often quite a challenge to make a 180 degree turn-around which is the end goal of *repentance*. But it's necessary to regularly reset our life-compass so that we face only toward Jesus. Only Jesus.[345] This prayer asks for precisely such an unexpected outcome, such unanticipated grace to begin again. It is not only possible but desirable for us to *expect a miracle,* to *expect the unexpected.* And Jesus in the Gospels encourages us to do just that, whether it suggests a minor or major revision of our lifestyle. How inspiring to reflect on the faith of Abraham and Sarah! Against all odds, their gift of faith led them to hope, and ultimately, to love.

---

[345] Mark 9:8 Suddenly when they looked around, they saw no one with them anymore, but only Jesus.

VISION

Saul, still breathing threats and murder against the disciples of the Lord, went to the high priest and asked him for letters to the synagogues at Damascus, so that if he found any who belonged to the Way, men or women, he might bring them bound to Jerusalem.[346]

That's a scary beginning, but fortunately Saul's encounter with the High Priest doesn't end there. Saul was literally hell-bent on snuffing out this upstart breakaway Jewish sect being called *The Way*. How dare they sport such an exclusive title! How dare they challenge the Law, the tradition, and *the* way it's always been done? "Well, I'm on *my* way," thought Saul, "to finally put an end to these rabble-rousing, wrong-headed rebels—these misguided traitors to the *true* Judaism!" Well, we've all heard about "the best laid plans of mice and men,"[347] haven't we? Perhaps we've also heard the Latin proverb *Homo proponit; deus disponat*, people plan, but God acts. What were Saul's plans as he rode out hastily after his interview with the High Priest? He was undoubtedly planning a murderous mission. But fortunately, God had other plans. One might say, it was high time for

---

346 Acts 9:1.
347 In the poem by Robert Burns, "To a Mouse," he refers to "the best laid schemes o' Mice an' Men."

Saul's *Come to Jesus* meeting. Saul really believed in what he was doing. He was sincere. There is no doubt about it. He was an "all or nothing" guy. Saul's personality type pressed the pedal to the metal, pulled out all the stops, and operated at highest intensity all the time. To say Saul was driven would be an understatement. To say he was an extremist would be closer to reality.

But still, God had other plans for Saul. And it was indeed time. And the way it all happened has become what we now call a *Pauline conversion*. Saul had always been a staunch believer in what he was doing. He thought he had perfect sight, 20/20 vision. He could see everything clearly. He had absolutely neither doubts nor qualms about his mission in life. But for a brief period, God took away his ability to see anything, so that he might see things differently, beginning to look with the inner eye of the soul. Seeing and believing usually go hand-in-hand. How often have we heard, "Seeing is believing?" Now, things had changed. Saul had suddenly become "blinded by the light," as a popular song went. What could he possibly learn, come to believe or embrace now that his physical sight had been taken away? Saul not only lost his sight; temporarily at least, he had lost his vision as well. God had already made plans. While Saul was in the throes of this transition, at the same time God was preparing Ananias for a special and challenging assignment:

> Now there was a disciple in Damascus named Ananias. The Lord said to him in a vision, "Ananias." He answered, "Here I am, Lord." The Lord said to him, "Get up and go to the street called Straight, and at the house of Judas look for a man of Tarsus named Saul. At this moment he is praying, and he has seen in a vision a

man named Ananias come in and lay his hands on him so that he might regain his sight."[348]

As a faithful and observant Jew, Saul was *praying*. During this prayer period he saw a vision of Ananias laying his hands upon him and healing him. But Ananias was painfully aware of Saul's reputation. Quite scared, he naturally reacted in fear:

> But Ananias answered, "Lord, I have heard from many about this man, how much evil he has done to your saints in Jerusalem; and here he has authority from the chief priests to bind all who invoke your name."[349]

Ananias was questioning, but not doubting, the Lord's words. One should note this distinction. Naturally, Ananias would be apprehensive about any interaction with this widely-feared man. His reputation preceded him. But even so, God still deployed a fearful Ananias to accomplish his mission, one which would soon change Saul to Paul:

> But the Lord said to [Ananias], "Go, for he is an instrument whom I have chosen to bring my name before Gentiles and kings and before the people of Israel; I myself will show him how much he must suffer for the sake of my name."[350]

What a dramatic turn of events! Zero to sixty and then back again. Ananias, a meek, obedient disciple living in

---

[348] Acts 9:10-12.
[349] Acts 9:13-14.
[350] Acts 9:15-16.

Damascus where Saul happened to be headed, is willing to become an instrument in God's hands. And because he said yes, the former persecutor Saul would be enabled to become the future Apostle Paul. Some theologians have suggested that without Paul, *the Way* would have quickly died out, as did other offshoots of traditional Judaism. By virtue of the interaction between Paul and Ananias, the life rhythms of both men would be unalterably changed. Before being apprised of God's plan for him, Ananias was essentially a nobody, someone who'd never been heard of before. A humble little guy, probably an introvert afraid of his own shadow, Ananias had probably been a mono-dimensional believer who'd never explored the depths of his faith. By agreeing to cooperate with God's plan, however, he grew significantly stronger. By accepting God's call to mission, his faith now came alive.

Saul's life had likewise become unalterably changed. For a brief period, he had gone from sixty to zero because of his temporarily imposed blindness. His all-out persecution of members of *The Way* had necessarily come to a screeching halt. After his miraculous healing at the trembling hands of a perfect stranger, Paul was now empowered to resume his customary velocity from zero to sixty, to ninety, and beyond, but this time impelled by the healing power of Jesus rather than by the diabolical spirit of hatred. Such reversals of fate, such radical turn-arounds, such *metanoia* moments find beautiful expression in the psalms:[351]

> You brought me up, O LORD,
> from the dead; you restored my life as
> I was going down to the grave.

---

[351] Psalm 30: 3, 5-6, 12.

> For his wrath endures
> but the twinkling of an eye,
> his favor for a lifetime.
> Weeping may spend the night,
> but joy comes in the morning.
>
> You have turned my wailing into dancing;
> you have put off my sack-cloth
> and clothed me with joy.

Reversals seem to abound for those who go from death to life, from wrath to favor, from weeping to rejoicing, from wailing to dancing, from sack-cloth to exquisite vesture. For newly-christened Paul, life went from hatred to love. And for Ananias, life went from timid obscurity to celebrated accomplishment. Such are the drastic, life-altering events which characterize Resurrection Life. Just plain *hearing* gives way to *listening*, and routine *seeing* becomes intentional *looking*. Sight is one thing, but vision is quite another.

VISITING

One of the most enjoyable holiday traditions for me is being with friends, throwing or attending dinner parties, and in general, just gathering with family and friends for some good conversation. I just love visiting. Being an off-the-charts extrovert by nature, I relish getting together with people, be they total strangers or old and dear friends. Whether at church, at home, in a coffee shop, or wherever else people gather. During the Covid-19 pandemic, of course, all bets were temporarily off. I suddenly turned into a a part-time cloistered monk. But there always existed the hope that eventually things would get back to normal.

Well, there are actually a number of expressions to express *getting together* with others. You can make a *visit* or go *visiting*. Ecclesiastically speaking, however, whenever a bishop, an archdeacon, a canon to the Ordinary or a regional dean *visits* a parish, such a *visit* gets a slight terminological upgrade. One ought properly refer to that event as a *visitation* rather than a *visit*. But those distinctions aside, how might we describe the concept of a *visit* versus that of a *visitation* in Holy Scripture?

In the first chapter of Luke, there are some encounters we might call *visits* and others we might term *visitations*. Well, who's visiting whom? And how did such encounters unfold? The first chapter of Luke, the gospel writer who renders the most robust *infancy narrative*,[352] chronicles the events leading up to the birth of Jesus. In this chapter, Luke records two angelic *visitations*. And these are not events where some ordinary, garden-variety angel shows up. No, an *arch*angel arrives here. What's the difference? An *arch*angel is somewhat like an *arch*bishop or an *arch*deacon when they make a *visitation* to a local parish. The prefix *arch-* implies *first* or *original*. Gabriel was one of the first angels created and therefore ranks very highly. In Luke's view, no lesser luminary would suffice. The most breaking news ever was to be delivered: the Messiah's birth announcement.

Gabriel's first visitation was to good *old* Zechariah. His wife Elizabeth was at least as superannuated as he, if not more so. These were no millennials, nor even Gen-Xers. They'd lived a long while. Zechariah was a Jewish priest. They had so many in those days that each would be assigned temple duty only a few days a year. And, as fate would have it, one of Zechariah's days turned out as anything but ordinary. Who would show up but the Archangel Gabriel, and completely unannounced!

Unfortunately for this temple priest, this would not turn out to be one of his better duty days. His reception of Gabriel was standoffish, distanced and cool, to put it charitably! When his angelic visitor revealed that he was to become a father,

> Zechariah said to the angel, "How can I be sure this will happen? I'm an old man now, and my wife is also well along in years." Then the angel said, "I am Gabriel! I stand in the very presence of God. It was he who sent me to bring you this good news! But now, since you didn't believe what I said, you will be silent and unable

---

352 Matthew, Mark and John go into less detail than Luke.

to speak until the child is born. For my words will certainly be fulfilled at the proper time."[353]

Zechariah's response lacked one essential element: trust. Maybe he was gripped by fear, but Gabriel discerned that Zechariah seriously doubted God's message. One doesn't treat an archangel or an archbishop that way and emerge unscathed. For his insolence Zechariah was silenced. He was tongue-tied until his son, John the Baptist, would be born nine months later. And then, on John's presentation and dedication in the temple, Father Zechariah would have something to sing about, and that has remained the beautiful canticle the *Song of Zechariah*.[354]

Gabriel's second visitation was to a much younger person than Zechariah. She was likely a teenager or perhaps a preteen. Happily, that interaction unfolded quite differently:

> In the sixth month of Elizabeth's pregnancy, God sent the angel Gabriel to Nazareth, a village in Galilee, to a virgin named Mary. She was engaged to be married to a man named Joseph, a descendant of King David. Gabriel appeared to her and said, "Greetings, favored woman! The Lord is with you!"[355] Confused and disturbed, Mary tried to think what the angel could mean. "Don't be afraid, Mary," the angel told her, "for you have found favor with God! You will conceive and give birth to a son, and

---

[353] Luke 1:18-20.
[354] Luke 1:68-79. This canticle or "little song" is traditionally recited as part of the liturgy of Morning Prayer.
[355] Gabriel's greeting is the biblical source for the opening words of the *Hail Mary*.

you will name him Jesus. He will be very
great and will be called the Son of the
Most High. The Lord God will give him the
throne of his ancestor David. And he will
reign over Israel forever; his Kingdom will
never end!" Mary asked the angel, "But
how can this happen? I am a virgin. "The
angel replied, "The Holy Spirit will come
upon you, and the power of the Most
High will overshadow you. So the baby
to be born will be holy, and he will be
called the Son of God. What's more, your
relative Elizabeth has become pregnant
in her old age! People used to say she was
barren, but she has conceived a son and
is now in her sixth month. For nothing is
impossible with God." Mary responded,
"I am the Lord's servant. May everything
you have said about me come true." And
then the angel left her.[356]

Gabriel interpreted Zechariah's and Mary's response to be as different as night and day. Even though frightened and confused, Mary remained humble, respectful, and receptive to the message, even though on a purely rational level, it made absolutely no sense at all. In the presence of an archangel, Mary was disposed to set human logic aside and simply trust what she was hearing. Her adventure continues.

> A few days later Mary hurried to the
> hill country of Judea, to the town where
> Zechariah lived. She entered the house
> and greeted Elizabeth. At the sound of
> Mary's greeting, Elizabeth's child leaped

---

[356] Luke 1: 26-38.

> within her, and Elizabeth was filled with the Holy Spirit. Elizabeth gave a glad cry and exclaimed to Mary, "God has blessed you above all women, and your child is blessed."[357]

Elisabeth, in her excitement, goes on to tell Mary:

> Why am I so honored, that the mother of my Lord should visit me? When I heard your greeting, the baby in my womb jumped for joy. You are blessed because you believed that the Lord would do what he said.[358]

Elisabeth's final comment holds the key for us to discern the stark difference between Mary's response and Zechariah's.

This Spirit-filled *visit* between two cousins reveals the core theological principle that "divine reality supersedes human logic." Judging purely on the basis of human logic, neither the very old nor the very young beget children, unless something special happens, unless there is divine intervention. The birth of John the Baptist as well as that of Jesus Christ both qualify as miracles, events where God has intervened. Each in its own right defies the laws of nature. And therefore, that's why in church-speak we refer to Mary's meeting with Elisabeth as the *Visitation* rather than simply the *Visit*. Mary did not simply drop-by. This was a significant and special encounter between two women, both "born for us and for our salvation."[359] While Gabriel's dialogue with Zechariah went awry, his Annunciation to Mary on the other

---

[357] Luke 1:39-42.
[358] Luke 1:43-45. Elizabeth's response to Mary is also the biblical source for the second half of the *Hail Mary*: "Blessed art thou amongst women, and blessed is the fruit of thy womb, [Jesus]."
[359] The Apostles' and the Nicene Creeds.

hand went beautifully. The Archangel encountered before him a humble, willing, and trusting soul who self-identified as a "handmaid of the Lord."[360] A little girl from a no-name village had agreed to become for the universal Church both *theotokos* as well as *mater Dei*.[361]

In one sense, today's story doesn't end with Gabriel's visitation either to Zechariah or Mary. It's really more about inviting us to ponder how *visitation* might take place in us. From my own personal perspective, how do I view the spiritual realm? Do I identify more closely with Zechariah or with Mary? Would I respond skeptically or positively if I were to encounter some manner of celestial visitation? It probably wouldn't match the drama in the first chapter of Luke, but how open am I to God visiting me any way God chooses?

> Purify our conscience, Almighty God, by your daily visitation, that your Son Jesus Christ, at his coming, may find in us a mansion prepared for himself; who lives and reigns with you, in the unity of the Holy Spirit, one God, now and for ever.[362]

---

[360] Luke 1:38: Then Mary said, "Here am I, the servant of the Lord; let it be with me according to your word." *Ecce ancilla Domini. Fiat mihi secundum verbum tuum.*
[361] The Western, Latin rite Church refers to Mary as the *Mater Dei*, Mother of God, whereas the Eastern rite more often sees her as *theotokos* or God-bearer.
[362] Collect for the Fourth Sunday of Advent, *BCP 1979*, p. 212.

Some Final Thoughts and Prayers

Dear Fellow Traveler,

Let's keep on looking for God in all the labyrinthine nooks and crannies of life, *in good times and bad*. Remember, as Peter pointed out, God shows no partiality, plays no favorites, but accepts anyone trying to do the right thing.[363] As these pages draw to a close, let us give thanks for the opportunity to spend time together in reflection. As we continue along the ever-surprising path of pilgrimage, let us pray that, among other things,

- our journey to the tomb may be a beginning, not an end;
- our pilgrimage be commencement, never simply graduation;
- we discover even more creative ways to apply these reflections;
- we keep seeking more conscious contact with God;
- we continue to seek the peace that passes human understanding;
- together we shout *Amen, Alleluia!*

---

[363] Acts 10:34.

About the Author

John Crean, born in New York City, grew up in Westchester and Southern Connecticut. Educated on the East Coast, he graduated from Fairfield Prep and Holy Cross College in Worcester, majoring in German, philosophy, and theology. John then received his master's and a doctorate in German at Yale. He taught there, then at the University of Wisconsin, the University of Hawaii, and finally at Grand Valley State University in Allendale, Michigan. John has published, edited, or co-authored numerous textbooks, scholarly articles, and books.

While teaching in Hawaii, John was also ordained an Episcopal priest. He continued from then on to serve bi-vocationally, holding both ecclesiastical as well as academic positions in Hawaii and Michigan.

Since 1980, John has presented and published on the *Rule of Benedict*, also serving as a coeditor and board member of *Magistra: A Journal of Women's Spirituality in History*. Appointed scholar-in-residence at the Huntington Library in San Marino, CA, John continued to research and publish on ecclesiastical history.

In 2020, Church Publishing, Inc. brought out his most recent book, *Recovering Benedict*, a daily devotional, blending the *Rule of Benedict* with the principles of twelve-step recovery. John currently resides in the Southern California desert, where he continues to write and assist at a local parish.

Follow John Crean:

www.jecjr.org

Facebook.com/100090360770372

www.ingramcontent.com/pod-product-compliance
Lightning Source LLC
Chambersburg PA
CBHW032222080426
42735CB00008B/672